HOW WARS BEGIN

The Italian Problem in European Diplomacy 1847–49
Germany's First Bid for Colonies, 1884–85
The Course of German History
The Habsburg Monarchy, 1809–1918
From Napoleon to Stalin
Rumours of Wars
The Struggle for Mastery in Europe 1848–1918
(The Oxford History of Modern Europe)
Bismarck: The Man and the Statesman
Englishmen and Others
The Trouble Makers
The Origins of the Second World War
The First World War
Politics in Wartime
English History, 1914–1945
(The Oxford History of England)
From Sarajevo to Potsdam
Europe: Grandeur and Decline
(Penguin: Selected Essays)
War by Time-Table
Beaverbrook
The Second World War
Essays in English History
The Last of Old Europe
The War Lords
The Russian War, 1941–1945

HOW
WARS BEGIN

A. J. P. Taylor

ATHENEUM NEW YORK
1979

To Eddie, their only begetter

Copyright © 1977, 1979 by A. J. P. Taylor
All rights reserved
Design by Patrick Leeson
ISBN 0-689-10982-2
Library of Congress catalog card number 79-84236
Typesetting and origination by Western Printing Services Ltd, Bristol
Printed in Great Britain by Ebenezer Baylis & Son Ltd,
The Trinity Press, Worcester, and London

First American Edition

Contents

Illustrations

11

Introduction

Six major wars have been fought in Europe since the French Revolution. A seventh was fought all over the world though Europe contributed to its outbreak and provided one field of combat. Since then there has been one major conflict which without leading to actual war had many of its characteristics. Two major wars—the American civil war of 1861 to 1865 and the Russo-Japanese war of 1904 to 1905, being fought entirely outside Europe, do not fall into the pattern of the others and I have therefore omitted them from my survey of how modern wars begin.

This has long been fertile ground for historians. Many of the wars had a long background or, as Renouvin wrote, profound causes. Two were presented as wars of creeds: the French revolutionary wars as a conflict between Jacobinism and reaction, the second world war between Fascism and democracy. The Austro-French war of 1859 and the Austro-Prussian war of 1866 were inspired in part by the principle of nationalism. Imperialist rivalries are often cited as contributing to the first world war. The overweening ambition of a single man —Napoleon at the beginning of the period and Hitler towards its end—has sometimes bulked large.

Public opinion, inflamed by a jingo press, has not escaped censure. Diplomats, too, have been made responsible. The first world war was widely attributed to secret diplomacy and to the European alliances that were its outcome. Militarism, preach-

13

ing the glories of war, has played its part. Sometimes, it is said, the guns went off of themselves. On a more prosaic level wars were allegedly provoked or at least encouraged by armament manufacturers, 'the merchants of death'.

Historians themselves might be added. In the nineteenth century, though perhaps less at the present day, they were fervent patriots, 'chaplains of the pirate ship' as Beatrice Webb called them. They presented the expansion of Empire as the noblest chapter in the history of their particular country. English historians glorified Queen Elizabeth I or the great Earl of Chatham; French historians glorified Napoleon I, though less unanimously; German historians made do with Frederick the Great or even Julius Caesar. On a slightly more academic level historians presented international relations as a series of conflicts between sovereign states, shaped by the ever-changing Balance of Power and leading inevitably, even admirably, to major wars.

All these explanations have some validity. But there is also another more prosaic origin of war: the precise moment when a statesman sets his name to the declaration of it. The statesman is no doubt a creature of his time and shares its outlook. But the actual act of signing his name has often little relation to the profound causes, as I discovered to my surprise when developing my theme. The Jacobins certainly hoped to carry the Rights of Man across Europe, but they were forced into war by the declared intention of the conservative powers to destroy the French revolution. Napoleon may well have aspired to found a great European Empire. But all his wars except the last were preventive wars, provoked by the preparations that others were making to attack him. The Japanese wished to dominate the Far East but they, too, were forced into war by the prospect that otherwise the American embargo on their oil would strangle them.

Public opinion has more often trailed after policy rather than determined it. Italian nationalists showed little enthusiasm for the Austro-French war of 1859 and German nationalists showed little for the Austro-Prussian war of 1866 until after Bismarck had achieved his victory. In 1870 Parisian crowds called 'à Berlin' only when war had been declared. In 1914 there were frenzied demonstrations for war in every European

14

capital again only when war had been declared. We have no idea whether they would have cheered as widely if peace had been preserved; British crowds certainly did so after the conference at Munich in 1938. The only case to be set on the other side is the Crimean war where popular hostility to Russia made it difficult for the British government to follow a conciliatory policy. Even so diplomatic muddle contributed more than an excited public opinion to the outbreak of the Crimean war.

Militarism, or rather the opinion of the military authorities, has of course always counted for something. Napoleon presumably knew what he was doing when he declared his wars, though in 1812 at any rate he judged wrongly. The Prussian general staff were confident of victory in 1866 and still more in 1870, though they did not actually provoke the declarations of war. The French generals should have advised against war in 1870 if they had understood their profession and instead urged war for purely emotional reasons. In 1914 all the general staffs reported that they were ready for war but only the German general staff pushed for its declaration and then at the last moment. Both Hitler and the Japanese intended to avoid a major war until later and were lured into it by the minor wars that they undertook. Perhaps the British and French general staffs of 1939 reported that war, though unwelcome, could be at any rate tolerated, but even this is doubtful.

Wars in fact have sprung more from apprehension than from a lust for war or for conquest. Paradoxically many of the European wars were started by a threatened Power which had nothing to gain by war and much to lose. Thus Austria started the Austro-French war of 1859 by her declaration of war on Sardinia. She started the Austro-Prussian war of 1866 by promoting the condemnation of Prussia at the Federal Diet. She started the first world war by her declaration of war on Serbia. Yet in each case she was almost bound to be the loser. Apprehension was reinforced by exasperation—with Austria the harassment of nationalist propaganda. Similarly France in 1870 was exasperated by Bismarck's successes and started the war by her declaration of war on Prussia.

England and France acted in much the same way in 1939 when they transformed the German invasion of Poland into the preliminaries of the second world war by declaring war on

Germany. The French expressed this when they said, 'Il faut en finir'. Even the Japanese acted more from apprehension than from aggression when they attacked Pearl Harbor in 1941. As to the Cold War between Soviet Russia and the United States, this seems in retrospect to have been motivated by mutual suspicion, at any rate for most of the time, rather than by any conscious design of one party to destroy the other.

Every Great Power is suspicious of any likely or even unlikely rival. What seems defence to one will always appear as an aggressive preparation to another. This has nothing to do with human nature which is infinitely variable. It is the inevitable consequence of the existence of sovereign states. Every Great Power relies on armaments as a means of deterrence. This deterrent has often worked and has given Europe long periods of peace. There comes a moment of impatience or misjudgement and the deterrent fails to work. With nuclear weapons the Balance of Power has been replaced by the Balance of Terror. This only means that the chances of war are less, not that they have been eliminated. In the old days the deterrent worked nine times out of ten. Now presumably it will work ninety-nine times out of a hundred. But if past experience is any guide—and as I have suggested in my conclusion it is not a certain one—the hundredth occasion will come.

Even so the nuclear weapons will not go off of themselves. In the last resort some human being will have to press the button just as in the past some statesman had to sign the declaration of war.

I presented this book as a series of impromptu lectures on BBC television in July 1977. The lectures now appear with tidier syntax and otherwise unchanged. I acknowledge with deep gratitude the support and guidance I received from Eddie Mirzoeff, the producer of the lectures. I also record thanks to Della Hilton, my secretary, who helped me to give them a readable form.

A J P Taylor

London

1
THE FIRST MODERN WAR

FROM FRENCH REVOLUTION TO FRENCH EMPIRE

The First Modern War

From French Revolution to French Empire

How do wars begin? This is perhaps the most constant theme of the historian. Wars make up most of European history. In every civilisation there have been wars, at any rate until, we think, our own time. Wars caused in all kinds of ways—wars of conquest, wars of imperial rivalries, wars of family disputes, religious wars.

In the eighteenth century they had settled down into almost legalistic wars, wars as to who had the right to the throne: the war of the Spanish Succession, the war of the Polish Succession, the war of the Austrian Succession, and indeed you could say in the early eighteenth century, though we don't call it such, the war of the English Succession which brought the Hanoverians to the throne. In the last two hundred years there has been a profound change. Wars have changed from being wars between rulers to being wars between nations, and it is these wars of the last two hundred years or so that I shall talk about. This was where modern history began. More than this, as I looked into the French Revolution and the wars that it caused, I realised that in some ways it was the most modern of all wars, a war brought about by rival systems of political outlook.

Undoubtedly, the French Revolution of 1789 was the most formidable event in modern European history. Charles James Fox said of it, and I think he was right 'How much the greatest event since the beginning of the world and how much the best',

The Pillnitz Conference, August 1791 (*left* Frederick William II, King of Prussia, *centre* Emperor Leopold II, *right* Elector of Saxony)

though not everyone would agree about the second part of the phrase. What made it so different? There had been revolutions, plenty of them, including incidentally a revolution in England which overthrew the monarch, but basically changes of family. The French Revolution was different because it brought into the world and Europe in particular, a new idea, the Rights of Man, and with the Rights of Man went the Rights of Nations. Where previously states had been based on dynastic power they were now based on national existence. In the old days, right up to 1789, a state was simply the property of its ruler; Madame de Pompadour called Louis XV 'France' even when she was in bed with him. Then suddenly there appeared the French people who said, '*We* are France'. This was a challenge to all the dynasties of Europe and there was a competition of propaganda and of assertion, with, as the French Revolution developed, first the liberal and then the radical, and then the revolutionary leaders staking out more aggressively the claims of the people of France and in time of course the claims of

Louis XVI announcing declaration of war at the Legislative Assembly, 20 April 1792

20

Valmy

others. After all if France had the right to be a nation, if France was composed of its peoples and not just of its King, this applied to others.

One of the factors which produced the revolutionary war was the provocative declaration which the French legislative assembly made on 19 November 1792, promising help and fraternity to every nation seeking to recover its liberty. The word recover is curious. Most of these nations had never had their liberty, but it was already a myth that there had been a distant time when peoples had all been free and had then been enslaved by their kings. In answer to this, or in rivalry to this, the kings and emperors of Europe had met as early as June

21

22

Execution of Louis XVI, engraving by Helman after Monnet

23

The Duke of Parma sees his paintings, including Correggio's 'St. Jerome', carried off by Bonaparte's officers

OPPOSITE

Desecration of a church during French Revolution, from the painting by Sweebach (Carnavalet Museum)

1791. They met at a place called Pillnitz and warned the French that, unless they behaved better, unless they treated their King better, the great powers of Europe would call them to order. The Declaration of Pillnitz marked the real beginning of the revolutionary war, because here were these kings seeking to display their authority, to rebuke the French, to push them back into discipline under Louis XVI. Instead it provoked them forward.

Something else was curious about it. Although two great forces, the one of monarchy, of tradition, of conservatism, the other of liberalism and nationalism, were moving against each other, neither of them looked at it in practical terms. The armies of old Europe, although they were competent professional forces, were not at all equipped to occupy a foreign country and to suppress it. They thought that warnings would be enough. For that matter with the revolution in France the French army practically collapsed and none of the violent statesmen who were preaching war or at any rate resistance to the rest of Europe had the slightest idea what the French army

25

was like. Each side thought that phrases would be enough. That is a common case before a war; that if you assert conservatism or revolutionary principles this in itself will shape things.

Strangely enough, though France was the one threatened, it was the French revolutionary government which finally plunged into war, declared war—threatened Austria in April 1792, and then actually went to war, though unable to do very much.

Why? Because as one of them said 'The time has come to start a new crusade, a crusade for universal liberty'. There was a more practical consideration. King Louis XVI was intriguing with the other kings, and the revolutionaries hoped that with war it would appear how he had been disloyal to his own country. The revolutionary leader Brissot said 'What we want is some great treason.' This worked. When the French revolutionary armies encountered the armies of the old regime and were defeated, the cry arose, as it does in a war, of 'Treason'. 'We are betrayed.' The very same cry that the French raised in 1940 when they were again defeated. People find it difficult to imagine that a defeat can happen for perfectly practical causes and not because of treason. At any rate Louis XVI was overthrown.

One date is memorable as the beginning of the modern world. On 20 September 1792 the French troops, who up to that time had hardly fought at all, stood in line at a place called Valmi where the Prussian army advanced against them. There was no really heavy fighting, there was a cannonade and for the first time the new French revolutionary troops did not run away. The Prussians pulled back and Goethe, who was with the Prussian officers, said 'Gentlemen, you have this day taken part in the birth of a new world.' Birth only, there was a great deal more to come. The French revolutionary wars were much more ragged than modern wars; they came here a bit and there a bit. It was not until the beginning of 1793 that this war began to extend all over Europe. Even then there was a great deal of muddle about it.

In 1792 the English government had claimed that they would stand aloof, since although England was not by any means a revolutionary country, she had a constitution and

26

Entry of the French into Milan, 1796

OVERLEAF
Napoleon's coronation as Emperor of the French

could not join with the absolute monarchs. At the same time
there was increasing apprehension, not only about France but
about the movement of revolutionaries and Jacobins inside the
country. There was an anti-Jacobin panic. After all, the greatest of all revolutionary statements of principle, the greatest
statement of democratic principles ever made, although it was
called the Right of Man, which was a French idea, was written
by an Englishman, Tom Paine. Increasingly the British government, faced with discontent and with demands for par-
liamentary reform, used France as the excuse for a policy of
repression. It is always tempting when you have political
discontent in your own country to say it is the fault of some

27

other country and not of your own government. Early in 1793 the British government demanded that the French revolutionaries should withdraw their support for peoples who wished to recover their liberty.

Two things marked the last days of January 1793, both of them assertions of revolutionary principle. Louis XVI was executed. Danton said 'The Kings of Europe challenge us, we throw down to Europe the head of a King.' It was defiance, a complete breach between revolutionary France and the traditional states of Europe, and at the end of the month revolu-

Plans for Napoleon's invasion of England

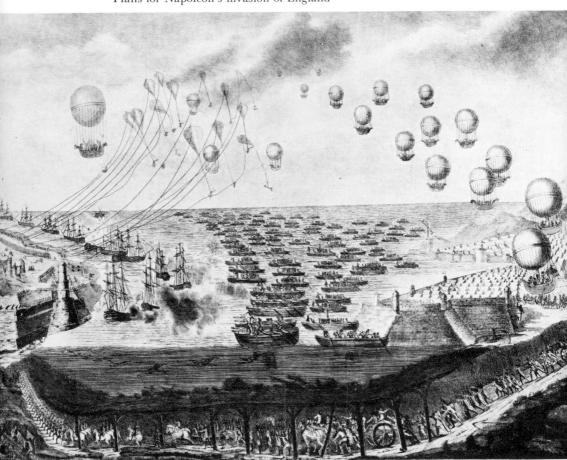

The surrender of Ulm to the French, 19 October 1805 (Carnavalet Museum)

tionary France declared war on Great Britain. This began the first of the coalition wars. It seemed to be a war of principles. On the one side the allies, the great powers, the kings and emperors were concerned or so they said to save civilisation, by which they meant themselves. The French revolutionaries were concerned to carry through new and universal principles of enlightenment. Never for a moment did they suggest that the Rights of Man were simply something for France. They were something for others and more than this—others must have them whether they wanted them or not. When the French invaded Belgium the Belgians deeply regretted that the churches were secularised and the monasteries and convents all closed. But the Belgians ought not to have done this; they ought to have welcomed liberation from the Church, liberation from their traditional rulers. French enthusiasm for liberty easily became French dogmatism for liberty.

On both sides also there were more practical considerations. When the allies started their crusade to save conservatism and civilisation, they also worked out the bits of French territory

31

The French invaders approaching Moscow

which they hoped to annexe. On the other side the French revolutionary armies, when they began to achieve victories, certainly brought with them liberation of a sort; liberation from the traditional institutions, liberation from the kings and princes, liberation from the Christian religion. At the same time they brought demands of a very practical nature. 'After all,' the French said, 'we have done the fighting, we have liberated you, we have presented you with the Rights of Man, we not only had to pay the money for these armies, we had actually to do the fighting for you as well. Therefore you must pay us.'

Wherever the armies of liberty went in Europe, they imposed indemnities. They collected so much so that there was a time when the French revolutionary wars were practically paying for themselves. Moreover as the armies grew greater and more powerful, the apprehensions of the civilian politicians in Paris grew greater also. What they wanted was that these revolutionary armies, splendid as they were in their spirit, devoted as they were to liberty and equality and fraternity, should not exert power in Paris itself. As one of the revolutionaries said 'We must get these scoundrels to march as far away from France as possible.' Revolution had become something for export.

So far as we remember these first wars at all, we think of them as one great block, a twenty year war which lasted from 1792 or 3 until 1814 or 15, throughout the nineteenth century it was called The Great War. But when I looked at it more closely I realised that it was not a continuous war, in a sense not even a continuing story. There were in this war two entirely different epochs which became confused afterwards but which were quite distinct. The revolutionary wars which asserted the independence of France and destroyed or at any rate defeated the crusade for conservatism and reaction, lasted a comparatively short time. By 1794 all the territory of France had been cleared. By 1795 France had reached what were called the natural frontiers. That is another curiosity by the way which was to be repeated all through the nineteenth century—the way in which a nation starts by claiming its national freedom, then says 'God or providence not only created this nation but created natural frontiers for it, and there they are.' Always, you

will find, natural frontiers mean more territory than you can claim for any other reason.

By 1795 France had reached the natural frontiers of the Rhine and the Alps. By 1796 the French armies had swept into Northern Italy and had established satellite republics there. This first wave of revolutionary wars asserting French power ended with the eighteenth century. There was a short and very important period of peace. In 1801 there was, although we forget it, universal peace in Europe, even England and France were not at war. And when war started again in 1804 it had taken a different character. The French revolutionaries who had conducted French affairs were replaced by a single man who in 1804 made himself emperor—Napoleon Bonaparte. The most powerful European emperor since Roman times. Napoleon achieved power not on a promise of universal war and conquest, but on the promise of restoring order.

When I looked at this history, the record of these Napoleonic wars, I realised how different they seem in the perspective of 150 or nearly 200 years. To those who experienced the wars and looked back to them they were purely wars of French aggression, or shall we say as many French people said afterwards, 'pure Napoleonic aggression'. After all, Napoleon's victories carried French arms and French authority right across Europe and historians have constantly speculated—what kind of an empire did he want to achieve? Surely he was aiming at some kind of universal monarchy?

But when you look at Napoleon's war in detail there emerges a striking contradiction of the traditional story. I hesitate to say this because if you venture an opinion of this kind and say 'well it really wasn't Napoleon who started these wars', this is felt to be somehow heterodox and provocative. But I think that is how it was.

Take the first of them, the war which was resumed between England and France after a very brief period of peace just when Napoleon had become emperor. What was the technical reason? The technical reason may not be why a war starts but it is at least the spark. The technical reason was simply this: that

Napoleon watching the burning of Moscow from the Kremlin (engraving by Cruikshank)

during the revolutionary war the Royal Navy occupied Malta. It was not theirs, it was not British, if anything it belonged to the Knights of Malta who had been there for the last 400 years and one of the terms of the Peace of Amiens between England and France was that the British would give up Malta. When the time came they refused to do so. They said to Napoleon 'you have not withdrawn from certain territories you have occupied in Europe—therefore we are going to stay in Malta'. The British are entitled always to mistrust other people but others are not entitled to mistrust the British. That is why England is known or was known abroad as 'Perfide Albion', because the British have two standards, one for themselves and one for other people.

This was the actual origin of the renewal of the war. And from this time on it was British policy to stir up new coalitions against Napoleon. The British had much more gold than anyone else and used it to ensure that the Austrians or the Prussians or whoever it might be, did the fighting. The French used to refer to these subsidies as 'the Cavalry of Saint George'. Right at the beginning of these ten years, the pattern was set for wars which occured at regular intervals. British attempts to create a coalition; Napoleon partly with his instinctive shrewdness, partly with his greater intelligence service, getting his blow in first. One of the things that the British greatly objected to about Napoleon, was that just when they were conspiring to produce a coalition against him, he would destroy the coalition instead before it was ready. Unfair, it was often claimed to be, that Napoleon moved too fast.

The first and most dramatic occasion was in 1804 when Napoleon had assembled 'the Army of England' with which he proposed to cross the Channel and occupy London. The project was not going well. Napoleon had not got command of the seas, in fact he was very soon to lose command of the seas altogether. And while the French army was still at Boulogne Napoleon heard that an Austrian army, propped up by British subsidies, was being built up on the Danube. He broke camp, the entire 'Army of England' moved across Europe— remember it was a much more formidable thing in those days; no railways, indeed not very good roads. And yet Napoleon, entirely under his own direction, was able to carry this army

Bonaparte's flight in disguise from his ruined Grand Army in Russia, from a
contemporary engraving

right across Europe and to surround the Austrian army at Ulm
in October 1805, before the Austrians knew that he had even
left Boulogne. In the further battles that followed, the coalition
crumbled. The story was repeated in 1808, a second Austrian
army accumulated, a second Austrian army surprised. The
Napoleonic empire was carried across Europe by war, not
because this was the aim, but because this was its result.
Napoleon was left more and more as the dominant factor in
Europe simply because he had to defeat the other countries
which were conspiring against him. It would be foolish to
suggest that Napoleon was a man of peace or of kindly, gentle
nature. Nevertheless in 1805, in 1808 and, should one say in
1812, he was provoked into war. The last and most dynamic of
the wars followed on Napoleon's decision to invade Russia.
Statesmen often decide to invade Russia. And when they do it
is always the same puzzle, why on earth did they do it? Russia
was remote from Europe. The idea that Russia would join in to
Europe and take part in these conspiracies, though the Russians had taken part in the coalition of 1805, seemed a little
speculative. Napoleon absolutely dominated Europe, could he
really believe that Russia would raise Europe against him? Not
at all, in fact he claimed he was going to Russia simply in order

37

The return of King Louis XVIII, 8 July 1815

to win the friendship of Alexander, the Tsar. His other idea was that once he had taken Moscow he would march straight on to India, which I think was a bit ambitious.

This was the first time when Napoleon deliberately decided to take the offensive, to commit an act of aggression without suspecting any coalitions or combinations, conspiracies against him. And it was 1812 which, again for the first time, produced universal European war. Up to this time there had been little patches here and there, they got bigger and bigger. 1812 produced first of all Napoleon's arrival in Moscow, he spent weeks there waiting for the Russian emissaries to come and make peace, but none came. Even then, this was still a war only between France and Russia. But with Napoleon driven out of Moscow, driven out of Russia, there came a coalition of the conservative European powers against him. So what we think of as the great war of all the powers involved, was a very short war between 1813 and 1814, and incidentally of course, the British contribution was always peripheral, on the edge. The British army in Spain did not arrive in France until Napoleon had already been defeated.

There was an epilogue after Napoleon had been exiled to Elba, the last of the Napoleonic wars which started simply because Napoleon turned up and said he wanted to be emperor again. At which all the powers of Europe put him to the ban of Europe and declared that he was an international criminal. And it was with this which we remember as the wonderful battle of Waterloo that the Napoleonic wars ended.

In appearance it seemed that nothing had been achieved by this twenty years of fighting, that the old order had been restored, and the rights of man forgotten. But all the same something had been achieved. It was for a very short period that, as Elizabeth Barrett Browning said '. . . kings crept out to feel the sun again'.

2
TWO CONTRASTING WARS

CRIMEA—THE DIPLOMATIC WAR
ITALY—THE WAR OF LIBERATION

Two Contrasting Wars

Crimea—The Diplomatic War
Italy—The War of Liberation

The Crimean war is of particular interest to English people. It was the only European war that Great Britain took part in between the battle of Waterloo in 1815 and the battle of Mons in 1914. It was also incidentally the first war that left behind it memorials to the ordinary soldiers killed and not merely the generals who led them.

The beginning of the conflict was a rivalry between two sets of monks in Jerusalem over the keys to the Holy Christian places. France backed the Latin monks, the Russians backed the Greek monks.

As it was the Turkish government that had to allot the keys both France and Russia put pressure on Turkey. France sent a battleship through the straits to Constantinople and the Latin monks got the keys.

Russia sent an army to the frontier of Turkey and the Latin monks lost the keys or some of them.

The tension was mounting, each country putting on the pressure and each beginning to suspect the other. By this time it was commonly accepted by the British and French governments and by many ordinary people too, that Russia, this tyrannical power, was hoping to overthrow Turkey and establish control of Constantinople. On the other side the Russians were convinced that England and France were hoping to close the straits making it impossible for Russian trade or Russian ships to get out into the Mediterranean.

Members of the Society for the Protection of Animals weeping over the victims of
the Eastern Question, Charivari, August 1853

There was a competition of suspicion, both lots of suspicion mostly unfounded. Then the European powers, behaving sensibly, tried to settle the dispute and held a conference at Vienna of the five great powers involved, England, France and Russia, with Austria and Prussia. They reached an agreement, something which would satisfy the Russians, a legitimate Russian protectorate over the Greek church without interfering with the sovereignty of Turkey. Something went wrong. It has been well said that the Crimean war was caused by the fact that there was a telegraph line from most places to Vienna but no

Destruction of the Turkish squadron at Sinope
by the Russians

A Russian encampment at Tarem-Bourga in Turkey

telegraph line from Constantinople to Vienna. The five great powers had agreed, but they could not ask the permission of Turkey because they could not get to Turkey in time over the wires; it took something like a week or ten days to get a message through.

When the Turks saw the agreement, they said 'It won't do at all, this deprives us too much of our sovereignty.' It took another ten days for the message to come back. By this time Russia felt thoroughly cheated. The Russians had agreed to what the other powers in Europe had insisted on and now they were told they could not have it. They therefore moved a stronger army up to and even across the Turkish frontier.

Then something quite extraordinary happened. Turkey, the weak power, the power that was supposed to be on the brink of dissolution, declared war on Russia and moved the Turkish army up against Russia although there was no fighting.

The war had in a sense started. It had started without any serious consideration of what was at stake. The Russians had not the slightest idea that they were going to get involved in a war over the Russian protection of the Greek church throughout Turkey. It had been started to some extent deliberately by Turkey because the Turks thought, 'the more we can get the war going, the more England and France will get involved'.

The Turkish fleet in the Black Sea was a very creaky old fleet, quite unfit for action. The Russians came out from their naval base at Sebastopol and sank the entire Turkish fleet at Sinope. There was a tremendous outburst of public opinion in England. This perfectly legitimate Russian action of war against a country that had declared war on it was described as 'the massacre of Sinope'.

There were protest meetings all over England and demands for war. Here was something new in European history, a deep involvement of what was called public opinion. Perhaps it did not go so deep down into the population but it certainly existed.

The Crimean war indeed was the first was which was helped on by the newpapers. In earlier wars the newspapers had had to catch up afterwards. *The Times* in particular led public opinion and public opinion was led to believe that Russia was

48

The defence of Sebastopol

Commissariat difficulties. The road from Balaclava to Sebastopol at Kadikoi during wet weather

not merely seeking to encroach on Turkey or to destroy Turkey, but was seeking to be the tyrant of Europe.

In 1849 Russian troops had intervened to suppress the national revolution in Hungary. Russian troops held down Poland and also sustained the two reactionary powers, Prussia and Austria. Russia prided herself on sustaining what was called the Holy Alliance of Reaction. In England which was then in its liberal phase, it was widely believed that if Russian power could be destroyed then Europe would become free.

The other powerful factor making for war was the ruler of France, Napoleon III who had become emperor in 1852 and hoped, though with little justification, to repeat the successes of his uncle, Napoleon I, perhaps not by means of universal war but by establishing a great political influence.

Here were the two quite different factors pushing to war: in England the desire to see a movement of liberation and in Napoleon the desire to see a movement, maybe of European liberation, but one led entirely by himself.

The body which was most unwilling to go to war was actually the British government, or some sections of it. The Prime Minister, Aberdeen, was so determined to remain at peace that he refused to take any precautions and when in fact he had to lead the country into war, he believed he had committed a great sin. Later in life after he had retired, he refused to build a church on his estate because like David, he had committed a great sin and God had said: 'Thou shalt not build an house in my name, because thou hast been a man of war and hast shed blood.'

There was no consideration of what was at stake, or whether even after this first engagement they could not go back to the arrangement which had been made before, which did not involve anything about the break up of Turkey or indeed any Russian influence in Turkey other than that the Turks should show reasonable sympathy with the members of the Greek Orthodox Church.

The British and French had said they were going to protect Turkey. They had sent their fleets to the Near East and yet the Turkish fleet had been destroyed. The British and French fleets therefore went through into the Black Sea and issued an ultimatum, ordering the Russian fleet to withdraw to harbour

Landing beach in the Crimea

and not to come out again without British and French permission. This technically was the cause of the Crimean war as we understand it, that is to say in which the great powers were involved.

The Russian fleet, although in fact it withdrew to Sebastopol, did not respond to the order as such and in May 1854 the Crimean war was declared. Even then the war did not actually begin because although the British and French had got their fleets in the Black Sea, how could they get at Russia? They were maritime powers, Russia was a land power.

By August considerable British and French armies had

Camp of the Fourth Dragoon Guards in the Crimea

accumulated at Constantinople which needed no defence. There they faced the problem which often arises in war 'Where shall we go? What shall we do with these armies that we have brought here?'

They could not march over land all the way from Constantinople to Moscow. So they said 'Let's take Sebastopol.' This was the main Russian naval port. At the time it was ill defended and there were very few Russian troops there. The British and French said 'It will be easy, we shall take it in a week. Then we shall have a considerable military achievement and public opinion will be satisfied.' The British and French

54

Interior of the Redan after the Russians' withdrawal

landed successfully. They moved towards Sebastopol and did not move fast enough. In fact they were so pleased at landing, they thought it was not worthwhile to do anything else. Instead of its taking a week it took 18 months for the British and French to capture Sebastopol. That was the Crimean war.

What happened about the keys to the Holy places I have no idea, whether the Latins got them or the Greeks got them or they shared them. Whether the Crimean war helped to preserve Turkey I also have no idea, although Turkey still exists. But in one sense the Crimean war was of great importance. It eliminated Russia as a great power in Europe for many years to come. You could argue that until the outbreak of the first world war, indeed I would argue that until 1941, nearly 100 years, Russia did not count in Europe to anything like the extent she had counted before the Crimean war. This enabled Liberal movements which sought for national independence and freedom to go forward without fearing Russian intervention.

The whole balance, not so much military but political, was changed. The conservative, reactionary powers which stood in the way of German nationalism and Italian nationalism were now very much on the defensive. The principal consequence of the Crimean war was that the question of the unification of Italy could be raised. This produced the second war of the 1850s, the war with the humdrum title of the Austro-French war but one with very significant results for Italy and for the history of Europe.

In 1848, the great year of revolutions, the Italians had tried to liberate themselves. At that time Italy was divided into a great number of states and the whole of Northern Italy was inside the Austrian empire. Both Lombardy and Venetia were ruled directly from Vienna.

In 1848 there were risings everywhere. The Austrians were driven out of Lombardy and out of Venetia. The little kingdom of Piedmont, sometimes called Sardinia, sent its army to the assistance of the liberal nationalists and was defeated. Austria re-conquered Lombardy and Venetia and Austrian rule was restored. It was restored more harshly than before because now there was complete estrangement between the Austrian rulers and the Italian ruled.

There were new conspiracies, there were bomb plots.

Camillo Cavour

Austrian soldiers were shot at and killed. It is the kind of thing which happens under alien rule but the kingdom of Piedmont on its own was not strong enough to create Italy or to liberate Northern Italy. In 1852 Piedmont acquired one of the great statesmen of the nineteenth century, Camillo Cavour. He decided that the right way to unite Italy was not by national passion and idealism but by hard-headed diplomacy. He set out to win Napoleon III for the Italian cause.

Napoleon III on his side believed that a united or a liberated Italy would be a grateful client state and that France would be able to dominate the Mediterranean. Also he wished to repeat the achievement of his uncle who had set up a kingdom of Italy of a sort. Moreover Napoleon III as an absolute ruler had to establish a reputation. Although by no means a distinguished soldier or general, he wanted to show that he was.

Napoleon III and Cavour met more or less in secret at Plombières, a spa, with very good spa water which I can recommend. While they were drinking the spa water, they made a deal. France would join Piedmont and get the Austrians out of Northern Italy. In return France would be allowed to acquire what were called the national frontiers of Savoy and Nice which at that time belonged to the King of Sardinia.

They had agreed on the war. Their problem was how to get it. Wars are expected to have a technical legal cause. You have to have grievances, you have to have claims to territory but Piedmont had no claims to Austrian territory. By every treaty right in the world, Austria was the rightful ruler of Northern Italy. Any international tribunal would have been bound to say: 'Austria is totally justified. There is no conceivable maxim of international law by which Austria should be compelled to withdraw from Northern Italy, or for that matter that France and Piedmont be allowed to go to war with her.'

Cavour was a very clever man, he said he would provide some respectable cause of war, some frontier grievance. Napoleon III and Cavour racked their brains over the problem.

On the other side the Austrian government grew increas-

Emperor Napoleon III

58

ingly exasperated by the more or less open preparations that were being made. Here was Piedmont preaching nationalism, subsidizing Italian national propaganda in Northern Italy, providing a refuge for Italian nationalists who had to escape from Lombardy, even although Piedmont was a monarchy providing a refuge for Italian republicans.

There was a free press in Piedmont, the only one in Italy which talked in liberal terms. There was even a parliament, two chambers meeting in Turin and claiming to speak in the name of Italy. It was very exasperating for a great imperial government that it was now being challenged by a miserable little jumped up state and with the implication that Austrian government was imcompetent and tyrannical. The Austrians had insisted that because they had legitimate right behind them they were the moral party. Now it was being suggested that for an empire to rule over people of a different nationality was actually immoral. This was particularly dynamite for the Austrian empire because all its territories really were non-national. The emperor did not belong to any nationality, his statesmen did not belong to any nationality although most of them spoke German. They were above nationality and once you raised the cry of national rights and national freedom, the Austrian empire might well break up as happened indeed in 1918 for exactly this reason.

The Austrians, therefore, felt that they must not only stand out against these national claims but must get their blow in first. This is a fascinating paradox. Austria could not conceivably gain by war. Austria could not annexe Piedmontese territory, that would give her more discontented Italians. She was not likely to be able to annexe French territory. The Austrian line surely should have been to remain firmly at peace and to give no possible excuse or opening for war. Instead the Austrians began to speak in increasingly bellicose terms. Then rather as before the Crimean war, the other powers tried to prevent a war.

The British government offered to mediate. The British ambassador in Paris went to Vienna and discussed the estrangement between Vienna and Paris. The Austrians said that they merely wished to be left alone. The British ambassador took the message back.

The Battle of Solferino, 1859: The French Chasseurs d'Afrique charge the Austrians. Combined casualties in this bloody engagement c. 30,000

Then the Tsar thought he would like to play some part and proposed a European congress. A European congress was summoned though it never met. The Austrians mistakenly believed that European opinion was moving on to their side. They thought, if they got their blow in first, they would knock out Sardinia-Piedmont that this would solve their problem.

Just at this moment Napoleon III deserted Cavour and said 'We cannot risk a war, you must disarm.' While he was saying this in secret, the Austrians said it in public. They sent an ultimatum demanding that Piedmont should disarm, without promising that Austria would do so as well. Cavour refused. The Austrians invaded Piedmont and were driven back. This was the beginning of the Austro-French war because France came to the aid of Sardinia-Piedmont.

How ironical that if the Austrians had waited another few days, Napoleon III would have compelled Piedmont to disarm and the Austrians would have achieved their aim. As it was they were defeated and lost Lombardy.

This is not the end of the story about the Italian wars of this time.

1859 was one sort of war. In 1860 there was quite another war, a war that does not come into the history books as a war. It was in fact the only guerilla war in history, or one of the very few, that succeeded. This was an unofficial war. Garibaldi

OPPOSITE
King Victor Emanuel II

Embarkation of the Thousand at Quarto, 5 May 1860

wanted to go somewhere to liberate some part of Italy. What he really wanted to do was to liberate Rome which at that time was ruled by the pope. He had defended Rome in 1849 at the time when it was a republic and he wanted to repeat his success.

Cavour was desperately anxious that Garibaldi should go somewhere else, anywhere rather than go to Rome which would cause an international crisis. Fortunately there was a peasant revolt in Sicily, such as there often were. Cavour persuaded Garibaldi to go off with a scratch force of 1,000 men, incidentally most of them middle class. When they were on their way, Garibaldi said to an Englishman: 'There is one

Garibaldi landing at Marsala

OPPOSITE
Garibaldi reaches Naples

curious thing about this expedition, I am the only working man on it.' I am not sure that he was a working man himself.

To everyone's astonishment this irregular force of 1,000 men managed to land in Sicily and overcame the army of the King of Naples which held Sicily. This army, seventy thousand men, were driven out by a thousand.

Now Garibaldi decided to go ahead again. At any rate he could get into Rome he thought from behind, by marching on Naples. He swept right through Naples and now there was the fear that he really would go on to Rome. The only way to stop him was for the regular Piedmontese army to come down, as an ally or as an antagonist, who could say?

It advanced down Italy and encountered Garibaldi just as he was preparing to march on Rome and at this moment he made his great sacrifice. Garibaldi was a republican but even more he was an enthusiast for Italian unification. He had fought for this cause. Indeed for its sake he betrayed the peasants whom he had inspired and led. He did not support their land claims. He was a man of the people. He felt deeply for them but the thing which was absolutely dominant in his mind was unification.

Garibaldi immensely distrusted and disliked Cavour but he had a curious sentimental attachment to Victor Emanuel II, the King of Sardinia-Piedmont, who was very much a man of Italian character. At this dramatic moment they met each other on horseback, Garibaldi at the head of his revolutionary

The meeting between Victor Emanuel II and Garibaldi at Teano

Garibaldi leaves for Caprera aboard *The Washington*

army riding north from Naples, Victor Emanuel II coming down from the north. Garibaldi rode up to the king and said 'Hail to the King of Italy'. With this, Italy was born.

On the way back into Naples, the King said 'How are you, caro Garibaldi?' 'Excellent, Majesty, and you?' 'Very well.'

Victor Emanuel asked Garibaldi what he would like: 'I will make you a duke, give you a great estate.'

Garibaldi said 'All I want is a bag of seed corn for my farm at Caprera' and with that he went back to his little farm.

Such are the things which make Garibaldi the most wholly admirable man in modern history.

Garibaldi at Caprera, 1865

3
BISMARCK'S WARS

Bismarck's Wars

In 1862 Otto von Bismarck became Minister President, Prime Minister that is, of Prussia and within the next few years Prussia was involved in three wars. I think one must call them Bismarck's wars although he was not solely responsible for them.

The first was a war by Prussia and Austria combined against Denmark over two duchies, Sleswig* and Holstein. Its causes were extremely complicated. Indeed Lord Palmerston said that there were only three people who could understand the problem. One was the Prince Consort who was dead; the second was a German professor who had gone mad, and the third was Palmerston himself who had forgotten about it. I think we had better leave it forgotten but it was a curious beginning; an alliance between Prussia and Austria, an alliance which was soon to be severed by Bismarck's own work.

Bismarck's achievement of course was to unite Germany. From 1815 onwards the German states were brought together in a loose confederation—something like the EEC, both in its complications and in its ineffectiveness.

Technically Austria was the presiding power, Prussia though a great power had to play a secondary part. For German Liberals and Nationalists this was an exasperating situation. The German Confederation had been created by the

* The old English fashion, which avoids favouring either the German or the Danish spelling.

70

Bismarck, 1870

Congress of Vienna. It was a part of international law and while it was easy for a revolutionary like Garibaldi in Italy to defy international law and make Italy, it was very different for Bismarck who was a conservative and the leading minister of a very conservative king.

Bismarck's achievement was to maintain conservative principles without abandoning the aim of liberal unity. What Bismarck would have liked, I think, was to reach a peaceful agreement with Austria. After all circumstances often change, despite international law, and circumstances had changed since 1815. In 1815 at the time of the Congress of Vienna Austria was the greater power and an empire, whereas Prussia was only a kingdom.

By the mid-1860s Austria had fallen behind. Prussia had become the greater power, greater in wealth and greater in industrial resources. Prussia was a prospering modern king-

Sleswig-Holstein War; after the storming of Dueppel

King William I of Prussia meets the Emperor Franz Joseph at
Gastein, August 19th, 1865

dom. Austria was a decaying or stagnant empire. Maybe the
wise course for a stagnant empire is to hitch itself on to some
other great power rather than run into troubles but it is very
difficult when you have been one of the greatest powers in
Europe to renounce some of your grandeur and step down. The
Austrian statesmen and the Austrian emperor, Franz Joseph,
were well aware of Austria's problems, conflicts of nationalities
and an ineffective economic system, and Austria's weakness in
Europe.

The Austrians had relied on allies, principally on Russia but
Russia had ceased to count in Europe after the Crimean war,

The war of 1866; the Eleventh Westphalian Hussars leaving Düsseldorf

and Great Britain who at one time had called Austria 'the natural ally' had also lost interest in Europe. Austria was very much on her own with the exception of France and here was another problem: Napoleon III, the semi-revolutionary emperor could not make up his mind whether he was on the side of the conservative power or on the side of the liberal and quasi-national power.

There is one other point to bear in mind; Austria depended essentially on her army. In 1848 at the time of the revolutions the great Austrian poet Grillparzer, addressing Radetzky, the Commander in Chief in Italy, wrote 'In deinem Lager ist Österreich.' In your military camp lies Austria. To confess the weakness of the army would be to confess a weakness of the monarchy altogether.

Departure of Austrian reserves, 1866

Central Depot for wounded soldiers, Austro-Prussian war, 1866

From 1864, the time of the Danish War, for the next two years there was ceaseless diplomatic manoeuvring between Bismarck on the one side and the Austrian statesmen on the other.

Bismarck gave the impression, as many people do when they are seeking a gain, that he was the conciliatory one. He offered compromises, he offered to sustain the Austrian empire elsewhere in Europe if Austria would renounce her position in Germany.

The Prussian victory at Sadowa, August 1866

He expressed a solidarity with conservative principles but at the same time he was always demanding that Austria should recognise equality between Prussia and Austria. If not, he threatened, there would be a Liberal revolutionary nationalism in Germany which would destroy both the conservative Prussian kingdom and the empire of Austria.

These negotiations had the strangest twists. In the middle of 1865, the King of Prussia and his ministers met at Gastein and held a council of war to decide whether they should go to war with Austria the next week. The delightful thing about it is that Gastein was actually in Austrian territory. Fancy going on holiday in your enemy's territory and discussing whether you should go to war with him. That is how they did things in those more or less civilised times.

The situation grew tenser and the problem—Cavour had it also in Italy but Bismarck had it much more—was how without infringing international law it was possible to challenge a system, such as the German Confederation, set up by international law. The only hope was that the country which benefited from international law, in other words Austria, could be herself provoked into war and Bismarck's persistent offers of peaceful settlement were, I think, intended to push the Austrians into impatience.

There is another fascinating thing: this was the first time that the actual time of mobilisation came to count. Instead of armies acting once a war had been declared, it was the movement of armies which brought the war on.

The technical point was this. The Prussian army could mobilise in three weeks, the Austrian army took six weeks, therefore unless Austria started to mobilise first she would be at a disadvantage. But if she mobilised first she would appear to be the aggressor so the Austrians tried to turn the trick by offering simultaneous disarmament. The King of Prussia thought he was caught and agreed. Bismarck was heartbroken, he had missed his war.

Then the Austrians were afraid of Italy in their rear: if they disarmed then perhaps Italy would attack them. They considered partial mobilisation. Then they said 'if we do partial mobilisation we shall not be able to have full mobilisation'. So they mobilised fully. When Bismarck heard this he exclaimed

Bismarck and Napoleon III at Biarritz

Queen Isabella II of Spain

82

'God Save the King' because from that moment William thought that Austria was the aggressor. Even then though Austria was mobilising, the Prussians could sit back for a fortnight and let Austria mobilise and thus appear to be the aggressor and still with their three weeks to catch up. As a matter of fact, all this business about a mobilisation race turned out to be pointless because both sides were fully mobilised when the war of 1866 began.

In the end, at the beginning of July 1866 the Austrians lost patience. They took the first step to war by getting the German Confederation to denounce Prussia. This gave Prussia the opportunity to withdraw from the German Confederation and declare that the Confederation was at an end. With that the Prussian armies could perhaps invade other German states but they had no real conflict with Austria. Indeed when it came to the point even Bismarck with all his ingenuity could not think of a reason why they were at war.

The Prussian army advanced through Saxony. When they reached the Austrian frontier, a junior Prussian officer was sent with a letter which he handed to the nearest Austrian officer. It said 'I beg to inform you that a state of war exists.' That is how one of the greatest wars of the century began, no ultimatum, no declaration of war, it just got going.

The war produced the desired result so far as Bismarck was concerned. Austria was excluded from Germany, northern Germany was put under Prussian hegemony and Prussia had become a greater power. Bismarck himself made a rather different comment, a comment which I think is particularly apposite to all the discussions which go on about war origins and about who is the aggressor, which country started it. When the King wanted to have revenge on Austria and said 'Austria started the war, therefore Austria should be punished', Bismarck replied 'Austria was no more in the wrong in opposing our claims than we were in making them.' That I think is all that there is to be said about charges of aggressive war or war guilt.

If ever there were a planned war, a war of purpose, it was Bismarck's war against Austria. That war had fulfilled a programme which the liberals had had for many years of virtually uniting Germany. It fulfilled Bismarck's programme because it had united or largely united Germany and established Prussian leadership in Germany without upsetting the conservative order. It had been a war defined in its purpose and limited in its achievement. The moment that Bismarck got what he wanted he stopped and although he may have hoped beforehand to get these results without war, possibly by bluff, possibly by negotiation, possibly by conciliation, at any rate it was quite clear in his mind that something like this was necessary if Prussia were to retain her leadership in Germany.

Relations between Prussia, or as it was now called, the North German Federation, and France were of quite a different character and although Bismarck was to be blamed for this war also, his responsibility was much less, responsibility at any rate only in the sense perhaps that he failed to foresee events. After all Prussia and France had no conflict. France technically at any rate did not claim to dominate Europe, let alone Germany. Prussia had no territorial claims on France. Any such claims sprang out of the subsequent war; they had not been formulated beforehand.

Napoleon III on his side had claims of a sort against Prussia and Germany. Napoleon III had been emperor of the French since 1852. He had arrived at this position largely because he possessed his uncle's name. As one of the great French historians said: 'His origins condemned him to success'. As a Napoleon he had to succeed, otherwise he would be discredited and people would say 'Why should we bother to have a Napoleon? We might just as well have a republic.'

He succeeded in Italy in 1859 when he had acquired Savoy and Nice, but he needed more success. He had a very enlightened view that France would be a stronger country if instead of divided countries there was a national Germany and a national Italy where they could all combine together. He was one of the many who saw a vision of a united Europe, a Europe which would be bound together on liberal national principles. He had welcomed therefore the national unification of Italy. He was not opposed to the national unification of Germany but there the other side of his position came in.

If Germany were to be united and stronger, then according to all the calculations of traditional diplomacy, France would be weaker and indeed Thiers, one of the French statesmen, said

Prince Leopold of Hohenzollern

Wilhelm I, German Emperor

Napoleon III near the end of his life

about the Prussian victory at Sadova in 1866 'It is we who
were beaten at Sadowa' because France was not now as strong
as when Germany was disunited. Therefore France should
receive compensation. Napoleon III duly demanded these
compensations and Bismarck very reasonably refused them.
There was no earthly reason why, because Germany had
become united, France should be compensated. The discussions tailed away, leaving resentment on both sides. Napoleon
tried by means of diplomacy, by threats of alliance, alliance
how paradoxical with Austria, the country which he had

turned out of Italy in 1859, or even alliances with both Austria and Italy to seek revenge, to hold up the advance of German power, to undo the unification of Germany which was now under way. None of these things achieved any success and the general impression of observers in the years before 1870 was that although Germany was not united yet because Southern Germany had not been brought in, she was on the move to unification and that Bismarck would accomplish the miracle of doing it not only without an international war but without social upheaval or revolution at home.

It was a slow process and Bismarck was perfectly patient and was prepared to wait. At the same time he was naturally anxious to increase the prestige of the King of Prussia. If the King of Prussia was to become the head of a united Germany, then he must rank along with the other great powers, perhaps take on an imperial name. This seems to be the explanation of a very strange story which started the conflict of 1870.

In 1868 there was a revolution in Spain. Queen Isabella was dissolute, she had been married to an impotent husband and took the not surprising way out of having many lovers who rather filled up the royal castle. In time the expenditure of maintaining these royal lovers exasperated the politicians. There was a revolution and Isabella was dethroned.

A Spanish general became temporary regent and there was a republic but the Spanish rulers did not want to remain republican and the throne of Spain was hawked around Europe. This raised a big problem. They did not want anybody who was too closely connected with any great royal house. Napoleon ran one of his cousins but there was a general outcry that this would be putting France in power in Spain. Then Bismarck had a bright idea.

Spain was a Catholic country. There was in the house of Hohenzollern, that of the Kings of Prussia, a separate family line who were Catholics. Now here was a young man, Leopold a prince of Hohenzollern who had all the qualifications. He was a liberal so that he would co-operate with liberal Germany. He was a good, loyal but not over-patriotic German and

Volunteering for the war of 1870, Paris (from a mural by A. Binet)

89

he was a Catholic, a beautiful answer you would think to the problem. Moreover his brother was already Prince of Rumania and had been nominated to this post by Napoleon III himself so obviously Napoleon did not dislike the Catholic Hohenzollerns.

Bismarck appreciated that there would be some French protests and he therefore meant to rush the thing. I should warn you there has been over 100 years of discussion and dispute and it is often alleged that Bismarck deliberately organised the Hohenzollern candidature in order to provoke France into war. It is also alleged that he did it in order to strengthen the German side against France during the war.

I think that these views are mistaken. Bismarck certainly said that if there were a Hohenzollern king in Spain, France would have to keep some army on the Pyrenees and this would make war less likely, not more so. He never imagined that Spain would go to war on the German side. So I think if anything his consideration was simply 'This will make France more reluctant to threaten us.'

It does not seem as if he was considering mainly this. He was considering largely the prestige of the Prussian royal house and also more practical things. He thought it would be good for trade between Germany and Spain because Bismarck was a very modern man and thought a lot about economics. He thought the Spaniards would be keener on buying things from German industry than French industry if they had a German king. The essential thing was to get Leopold to Spain and on the throne before the French could protest.

The Spanish representative in Berlin sent a telegram on 26 June 1870 saying 'I will be back in three days with Leopold's consent.' The Spanish Parliament or Cortes was in session; it would meet on 29 June; Leopold would be in and the French taken by suprise. But a cypher clerk in the German legation in Madrid read the cyphers wrongly. He reported that the Spaniard coming from Berlin would only arrive on 9 July. This was too long for the Cortes to wait during the summer heat and its members went away. By the time Salazar, for that was his name, arrived, the Cortes had dispersed. The members had to be summoned back. It had to be explained why they were being brought back; they were being brought back to elect a

90

Departure of King Wilhelm I for the army

king and therefore the news became public.

Leopold in fact never got to Spain at all. The surprise was never sprung. Instead the news arrived in Paris and there followed a decision which made war more than likely, inevitable.

The Bonapartist dynasty, Napoleon III and his family, were losing prestige. Napoleon III was harassed by the demands of Liberals to turn his empire into a constitutional monarchy. He had only a young son who was not old enough to take over from

Krupps' gigantic cannon on display at the Paris Exhibition, 1867

him. He himself was a very sick man; he died three years later and had been sick for a long time before that.

The tough old guard who had put him on the throne, the Bonapartist adventurers who had made a fortune out of the empire and were a set of scamps for the most part, were anxious to restore the prestige of the empire and how could this be done? Why, by humiliating Prussia. Far from hesitating and saying 'This is a plot of Bismarck's to catch us in a war' they—if it were a trap—jumped straight into it, they welcomed it because they thought they had a strong case.

If the French government had merely wanted to stop the candidature of Leopold, they could have protested at Madrid and it would have been dropped. But with this there would be no prestige, therefore they must protest in Germany, protest to

King William. The protest was made to the great delight of Napoleon III and his advisers.

William I who had disliked the idea of Leopold going to Spain all along agreed at once to drop him. The reason why William wanted Leopold not to go was not at all that he was worried about France but he thought Leopold might get killed and that in any case the job of being King of Spain was not an attractive one for a cousin of his. He said 'Gladly. I never liked the idea. I will have a word with the boy and he will withdraw.'

This was no good for the French ministers. They had not humiliated Prussia. Instead William I had been conciliatory and friendly. The French foreign minister therefore sent another note, insisting that William must apologise, although he never had anything to do with the candidature. Not only must he apologise, he must promise that Leopold would never try to run as candidate again. He must give guarantees that no such thing should ever happen again.

Bismarck had no idea that the war would blow up as it did

Prussian artillery besieging Strasbourg, 1870

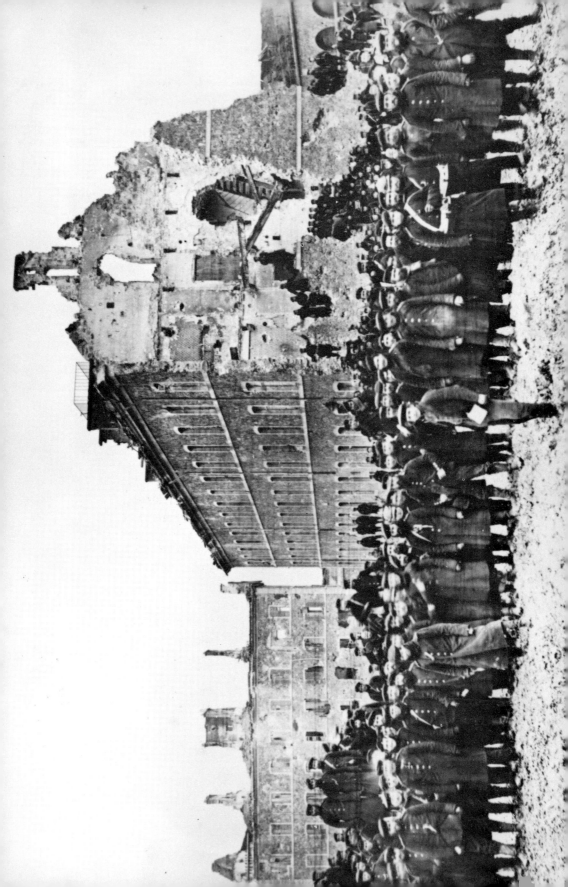

and was taken as much by surprise as everyone else. Bismarck was far away in the country. When the first French demand was made, he felt this was humiliating but he was rather relieved. Bismarck was a great one for putting the blame on others. Now the humiliation had fallen on William I, not on himself.

Just at the time when the second French demand was under way Bismarck came back to Berlin. He was depressed that he had missed a great chance. Prussia could have asserted herself by answering sternly. Instead the king had let them down. We have a description of Bismarck having supper with Moltke, chief of the General Staff, both of them very gloomy and speaking very unfavourably about William, about how feeble he had been just because of the threat of war or worrying over Leopold.

Then there came the second message from William, describing the meeting where he had been ordered to apologise. He had said, though in a very gentle way 'I told the French ambassador I had nothing more to say to him. Leopold has withdrawn. I have nothing more to say.'

Bismarck said 'That's it'. He seized a pencil and edited the king's telegram. It is called the Ems telegram because William sent it from Ems. Every word Bismarck put in the telegram was correct but it was arranged in such a way that instead of the King saying 'Well Leopold had withdrawn, there is nothing more I need to say', the King merely said 'I have nothing to say to you.' Bismarck's version was published the same day and with this the French press was in an uproar. The streets of Paris reverberated with the cry 'To Berlin' and Napoleon III prepared to go to war.

One extraordinary thing about this story is the total lack of consideration displayed by the French and by Napoleon III as to the possibilities of going to war. It seems very late in the day that men when they are moving on the edge of war, look at it and say 'Can we win, is there any sense in it?'

As a matter of fact the French army was in a very bad state. Napoleon III who had certain training as an artillery officer

Prussian troops at Fort Issy, 1st February 1871

Prussians attacking at the battle of Sedan

Napoleon and Bismarck on the morning after the Battle of Sedan (from a painting by W. von Camphausen)

was aware of this and reform of the French army had begun. This reform was still dragging behind. People earlier had despised the Prussian army. Its victory in 1866 showed that it was the first in Europe but when it came to the point, Napoleon and the Council of Ministers relied solely on their prestige, the prestige of the great name of Napoleon I. Thus for a cause which they themselves had trumped up they launched a great war in which France suffered defeat after defeat and at the end blamed Bismarck for it.

As for Bismarck, he drew a striking moral from having laid on three wars: to have no more wars.

4
THE FIRST WORLD
WAR

The First World War

The Great War, the first world war as it was later called, broke out at the beginning of August 1914 and it followed on a month of intense activity.

Indeed the month of July 1914 has probably been more studied than any other month in history. Thousands of documents have been published—British documents, French documents, German documents, Russian documents, Italian documents. Only the Serbs have not revealed their documents although they are said to be in print. Hundreds of historians have laboured, one book after another has been written.

During the war of course each side blamed the other. The Germans said it was caused by entente aggression planned by Russia or France. The allies said that it was caused by German aggression and the Treaty of Versailles repeated this statement.

Gradually, as historians worked, these sharp interpretations were rejected and there grew up something like a general agreement. There were still qualifications that one power had made more mistakes or was more at fault than the other but broadly by the time the second world war came along, historians were agreed that there had been no deliberate plan for war on the part of any power and that there had been a series of mishaps and mistakes and misunderstandings. As Lloyd George said 'We all muddled into war.'

Just when historians thought 'Well that is one subject I can

International Socialist Conference at Stuttgart, August
1907, including Georg Ledebour, Rudolf Hilferding,
Oskar Cohn, Karl Liebknecht, Ludwig Frank and (?)
Rosa Luxembourg (*seated second from right*)

talk on for ever and never have to add anything new' there
came along a German historian Fritz Fischer from Hamburg,
who studied first of all the German war aims actually during
the war. They were as you can imagine to hold on to all the
territory that they had conquered and get more if they could.
Then Fischer turned back to the period before the war and
identified these aims as having already been formulated,
perhaps not in the highest places but in very influential circles
where the talk was of the conquests to be made. Other historians joined him, some of them arguing that the Russian
army was outstripping the German and that the German
generals had agreed that in 1914 was the last chance when they
could fight a favourable war.

In recent years the younger generation of German historians
has come more and more to the belief that the Imperial Ger-

man government was actually a driving force for war and that the war which broke out in August 1914 far from being a war of accident was a war of design: a war, as one of them said, long prepared for.

The Imperial government, it was alleged, was anxious for war in order to prevent the victory of social democracy and the transformation of Germany into a democratic country. It was fought not only in the interests of the imperial authorities, the officers and the army, but of the German landed class. The historians who say this are not Marxists, they are historians from Western Germany.

In fact the Marxists in Eastern Germany are very jealous that they did not hit on this. They said of course empires cause wars but they had not done the work in detail; it was the development of purely liberal German historians. Others laid more emphasis on the military side, the actual fear that Russia was going to get too strong.

The only way one can answer this I think is to describe what happened or some of it.

On 28 June the Archduke Franz Ferdinand visited the town of Sarajevo in Bosnia. Bosnia is a Slav, Serbo-Croat province, only acquired by Austria-Hungary in 1908 and there was a good deal of discontent there. Franz Ferdinand did not however go there in order to make a demonstration against the discontent; he went because he had married beneath the permitted degrees. His wife was only a countess so she did not rank as an archduchess but if he went to Sarajevo which was still under military occupation he could go as Inspector General of the army and she would rank right at the top. It was to give his wife a treat that he went to Sarajevo.

The Serbian government certainly did not want to provoke a crisis, of that we can be quite sure. There were of course, as there have been in later times, plenty of national conspirators. Half a dozen of these were schoolboys working for what we now call their A levels. They said 'We ought not to let the archduke's visit go without some sort of demonstration.' Although they did not in fact belong to the secret society, the Black Hand, which was supposed to organise conspiracies, they got a couple of revolvers and a couple of bombs and they turned up on the day. As the archduke drove along, the first conspirator

102

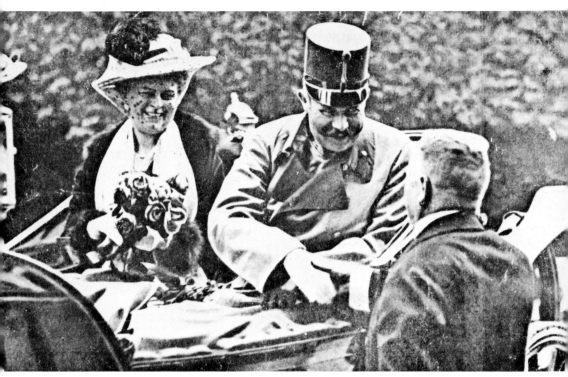

The Archduke Franz Ferdinand of Austria and the
Duchess Sophie shortly before their assassination
at Sarajevo, June 1914

could not get his revolver out of his pocket because the crowd
was too tight, and the second thought a policeman was looking
at him, the third felt sorry for the archduke's wife. The fourth
simply went home. The fifth threw his bomb which missed,
though it injured one equerry. The sixth, Gavrilo Princip,
having heard the bomb go off, thought 'Ah, it has succeeded'
and stepped aside. At that moment the procession drove by.
Princip realised that it had failed. He sat down in a café, very
gloomy.

The archduke drove on to the town hall, arrived in a great
rage and said 'I come here and you greet me with bombs. I am
not stopping, I am driving straight out. I am not going back
through the old town.' However the chauffeur had not been
told that they were driving straight on, not turning; when they
came to the turn where the original route had been, he turned;

and there was Princip sitting on the edge of the pavement in a café. To his astonishment he saw an open car with the archduke and archduke's wife stationary in front of him. He walked out of the café, stepped on to the running board of the car, took out his revolver, shot the archduke and then aimed at the Governor of Bosnia who was sitting in the front of the car and hit the archduke's wife who was sitting at the back. That was the assassination at Sarajevo.

An empire cannot allow the heir to the throne to be assassinated without doing something about it. The obvious thing to do

The Emperor Franz Joseph of Austria (1830–1916) before the coffins in the Hofburg of the Archduke and his wife

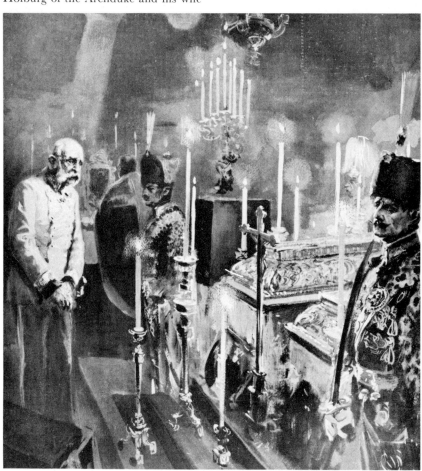

The Kaiser with a group of his generals on the last military manoeuvres before the outbreak of war in 1914

was to blame the nationalists and particularly to blame Serbia who really had nothing to do with it. The Austrian government were anxious to do this but they ran a shaky old empire and dared not go ahead without the support of their German ally.

An Austrian representative went to see William II the German Emperor at Potsdam. Nearly everyone had gone on holiday. All the generals were on holiday. Moltke was somewhere in the country having an agreeable time. William II himself was just off to the North Sea. However he had time to see the Austrian and in the afternoon, the Imperial Chancellor Bethmann Hollweg arrived as well. William, supported by Bethmann, gave a firm response: Germany would support Austria in her claims against Serbia and would stand by Austria even if Russia, the patron of Serbia, intervened.

Neither William nor Bethmann consulted a single general of

any importance. They did not turn to the general staff and say 'Is the time right for a war? How long do you want before there is a war?' More than this, William had never been told the earlier arguments such as they were. He had no acquaintance with the military details.

We have quite recently got some new information. Some-body has investigated the reports of the German military intelligence for the whole month which curiously no one had looked at before, and what do they tell us? They tell us that on 5 July which was when the meeting took place, military intelligence was not given any warning that war might be imminent. During the whole month of July German military intelligence recorded no special activities. No general was consulted, no troops were moved, no preparations for war were made. Indeed if this was a decision for war it was a very haphazard one and from what the reports of German military intelligence reveal, you would imagine you were in a completely peaceful country, as indeed I think you were.

There was then a long gap, very characteristically Austrian. Having decided to act at once against Serbia, it took the Austrians three weeks to draw up an ultimatum. One reason perhaps was that President Poincaré was visiting St. Peters-burg and the Austrians did not want a fuss while the French president was with the tsar. For another reason, the Austrians were solemnly working away, trying to discover and totally failing to find any kind of proof that Serbia had been involved.

In the end the Austrians felt that they really must do some-thing so they hotchpotched an ultimatum and sent it to Serbia. The Serb government was extremely anxious not to have a war, Serbia had just been involved in the Balkan Wars and the Serb army was in no condition for a war. Pasič the prime minister very characteristically said he was going on a holiday and would leave his colleagues to draft an answer. However at the last minute he was brought back and the Serb answer accepted every Austrian demand. Then before it was handed over, the ministers revised it and cut out a number of conces-sions. This is another puzzling little point. Why did the Serbs instead of simply accepting every humiliation alter the answer to the ultimatum so that it would be unsatisfactory? This we do not know. It is sometimes alleged that the Russians told them

Bethmann Hollweg, Imperial Chancellor

to do it because Russia wanted to provoke a war. There is no evidence to this effect. The Russian minister to Belgrade, Hartwig, had been in such a state of excitement over this tense situation that when calling on the Austrian representative he fell down dead. Thus Russia had no representative in Belgrade.

My own guess is that the Serbs wanted to prolong the negotiations. They thought 'If we accept everything then that will be it, but if we put in some hesitations then the Austrians will have to come back and make the demands again.' Instead of this the Austrians, knowing how dilatory and hesitating they themselves usually were, acted resolutely for once. The Austrian minister looked at the answers, said 'Not complete acceptance' and broke off relations.

At this for the first time there was a chance to negotiate. Sir

President Poincaré of the French Republic with Tsar Nicholas II leaving the landing stage at Kronstadt, July 1914

Edward Grey, the British Foreign Secretary, suggested there should be negotiations between Serbia and Austria-Hungary. To prevent negotiations, Austria then declared war on Serbia, fearful that if there were negotiations, concessions would be imposed on Austria as well as on Serbia.

Grey's line by the way was that all the concessions should be made by Serbia. He said 'Peace is more important than justice and therefore Serbia as the weaker power must give way.' It was fortunate perhaps that he never got the negotiations started.

The Austrian declaration of war on Serbia was pure theory; no action followed it. Now this gives the essential factor in the outbreak of the first world war. All the great powers, of whom

The Serbian Prime Minister Pasič

there were five, or six counting Italy, had vast conscript armies. These armies of course were not maintained in peace time. They were brought together by mobilisation. This factor had already counted before in the Austro-Prussian war of 1866, but this time there was a further complication.

All mobilisation plans depended on the railways. At that time the automobile was hardly used, certainly not as an instrument of mass transport, and railways demand time-tables.

All the mobilisation plans had been timed to the minute, months or even years before and they could not be changed. Modification in one direction would ruin them in every other direction. Any attempt for instance by the Austrians to mobilise against Serbia would mean that they could not then mobilise as well against Russia because two lots of trains would be running against each other. The same problem was to arise later for the Russians and in the end for the Germans who, having a plan to mobilise against France, could not switch round and mobilise again against Russia. Any alteration in the mobilisation plan meant not a delay for 24 hours but for at least six months before the next lot of timetables were ready.

The Austrians could not mobilise against Serbia because this would mean that they were defenceless against Russia so they did not mobilise at all.

The Russians then thought they ought to stake out some claim to prove that they were going to support Serbia so the tsar and his advisers contemplated mobilisation but only against Austria and this was actually ordered. Then the Russian generals who knew about the timetables pointed out that if they began to mobilise against Austria, they would then be totally defenceless against Germany because they could not then mobilise against Germany. Partial mobilisation was scrapped. The next day the Russian generals said 'But this is terrible. We have done nothing. Right, we will have general mobilisation.' They were still hesitating and the chief of the general staff himself said that this was rather pushing things beyond what they wanted. They had no idea of a war against Germany or even against Austria. They wanted a threat, not a real preparation for war. Mobilisation was a mere gesture.

The chief of the general staff rashly said in the tsar's presence

110

Sir Edward Grey

'It is very hard to decide.' The tsar who was one of the most weak-willed men there had ever been, was roused by this and said 'I will decide: general mobilisation.' He then, according to his diary, having made this decision, went out, found a pleasant warm day and went for a bathe in the sea. His diary does not mention mobilisation.

Now with Russia mobilising, the problem moved to Germany and here again this was entirely a matter of timetables. It was said afterwards that mobilisation meant war. Technically for most countries this was not true; it was merely a step towards war. Mobilisation after all took place within the country. The Royal Navy had mobilised as late as 1911. Russia mobilised in 1913. There were occasions when other powers had mobilised and because war did not take place the armies could be dispersed. With one country, however, this did not

111

apply. The German general staff ever since the creation of a united Germany in 1871 under Bismarck had contemplated the possibility of war on two fronts: France on the one side, Russia on the other.

It is the function of general staffs to plan for wars. Germany had two great neighbours, France on the one side, Russia on the other. Moreover in 1894, France and Russia made an alliance which was technically defensive in nature, that each would help the other if attacked. Thus Germany might have a two-front war. Successive German chiefs of general staff, Moltke, Schlieffen, the younger Moltke, all laid down 'Germany cannot fight two great wars at the same time.'

As often happens with chiefs of the general staff, they were quite wrong. In 1914 Germany fought a two-front war and continued to fight it successfully until 1918. This was a false

Count Alfred von Schlieffen

Mobilisation of the Russian army, Petersburg

alarm but it was an alarm which absolutely dictated their policy.

If you are faced with war on two fronts and have not got the resources to conduct both wars, what should you do? By definition you cannot eliminate one of the dangers by diplomacy because if you did there would not be a two-front war, in fact there would not be a war at all. You must assume that diplomacy has failed.

The German answer was to get in one blow first and so decisively that they would have eliminated one enemy. At first they thought of doing it against Russia, then decided that that was too difficult. Russia was too big; the German army would

113

114

French troops leaving for the Front, 1914

go rambling into far remote places. The other answer therefore was to eliminate France. Ever since they began planning this the idea had been 'We must beat France first.' But France had a strongly fortified frontier. After about 1890 the Germans decided they could not rush this frontier in the way that they had rushed the French frontier in 1870. A way round must be found and it must be through Belgium. The Germans arrived at this conclusion as early as 1893 although it took a long time before the full plan was developed. Its most detailed form was laid down in 1905.

German soldiers departing for East Prussia to resist the Russian invasion, 1914

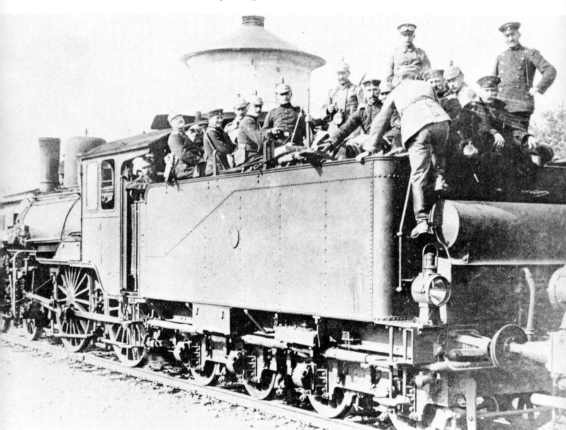

Outside Buckingham Palace at the outbreak of war, 1914

One essential part of this plan was to go through Belgium. The other essential part which was equally important was that there could be no delay between mobilisation and war because if there were delay then Russia would catch up and the Germans would get the two-front war after all. So the moment that the Germans decided on mobilisation, they decided for war, or rather war followed of itself. The railway timetables which in other countries brought men to their mobilising centres, in the Schlieffen Plan continued and brought the troops not to their barracks, but into Belgium and Northern France. The German mobilisation plan actually laid down the first 40 days of the German invasion of France and none of it could be altered because if it did all the timetables would go wrong. Thus the decision for mobilisation which the German general staff made and which Bethmann endorsed on 29 July was a decision for a general European war.

There was no deeper consideration in the background. Nothing was weighed except the technical point: if Russia

The British Expeditionary Force in Boulogne, August 1914

mobilises we must go to war. Serbia and Austria-Hungary were forgotten. The Germans declared war on Russia simply because Russia had mobilised.

The Germans were very stuck over France; they had no conceivable grievance against France. They demanded that France should promise neutrality, to which the French prime minister merely replied 'France will consult her own interests.' The Germans then invented an allegation that Nuremberg had been bombed by French planes. This was untrue. Whether there had ever been bombing I am not clear. It may be that a German plane had dropped bombs, but who did what did not matter; the thing was to get the war going. Thus the war came about mainly because of railway timetables.

There was one further and in the long run perhaps the most dramatic and decisive consequence. The continental powers were at war; Great Britain was not. The whole trend of British policy or certainly the desire of the British people had been to stay out of war.

The Liberal government asserted that Great Britain had given no pledges. In secret the British had already arranged a railway timetable to take the British army to the left flank of the French army but this had been concealed from the British public. Assertions were made constantly by the prime minister and by the foreign secretary that no commitment had been made which would limit the freedom of Parliament and the British people to decide.

Now this was very awkward because the French had been told over and over again 'Yes, yes, we shall stand by you if you are threatened by Germany' and the cabinet was divided. It looked as if the Liberal government would break up, perhaps the Conservatives would take over, there would be even more controversy than there had been during the Boer War, more than there had been during the revolutionary wars against France. Then came the news that the Germans had demanded the right to go through Belgium.

It is often said that this had been known for a long time beforehand. That the Germans had such military plans was indeed known, but the diplomatic consequences were not realised. Indeed Bethmann Hollweg himself, the German Chancellor, had no idea until 29 July that he would be setting his

Recruiting in London, 1914

name to a demand that the Germans should go through Belgium.

British Liberal ministers later on claimed that they had hung back and said 'Don't worry' because they knew Belgium would solve the problem. However it came as a complete surprise to most people and produced a tremendous reaction. Great Britain it seemed went to war, not in order to play a part in the balance of power, not in order to aid France or to destroy Germany as an imperial rival or to destroy the German navy. Great Britain went to war, in the phrase used from the very first, 'to fulfil her obligations to Belgium and in defence of the rights of small nations'. This did the trick in the House of Commons. It did the trick with British public opinion. In a sense it has done the trick with people ever since.

Very few people looked at the Treaty of 1839 which established Belgium as a neutral country. The guarantor countries were given by this treaty the right to intervene in order to defend the neutrality of Belgium. There was no obligation laid on them to do so. I am not saying for a moment that there was no obligation of a moral kind. Belgium was a small country and Belgium was very wrongfully invaded, just as for instance in 1916 France and Great Britain invaded Greece in exactly the same way, though with less fighting than when the Germans invaded Belgium, but the treaty obligation was something invented for the sake of public opinion.

All the great powers had relied in fact on the deterrent, the deterrent of great armaments. Previously the deterrent had worked. On this occasion the deterrent did not work and so it will be again.

5
THE SECOND WORLD WAR

The Second World War

The problem with the second world war is not so much how did it begin but when did it begin. The second world war was not some precise, sudden event like the first. The first world war as we now call it was perfectly simple in its beginning.

In July 1914 all the great powers were at peace and a month later at the beginning of August 1914 they were all at war, and you can really describe that, as I have tried to do, in terms of a week or a month at most. But the second world war, exactly when did it become a world war? When in fact did it become a war at all?

Suppose you said that a declaration of war indicates that the world war has started, then you would have to go back to April 1932 when Mao Tse-tung and Chu Teh declared war on Japan in the name of the Kiangsi Soviet.

For the Abyssinians the war started in 1935. For the Spanish Republicans it started in 1936; for the Czechs, even though they were defeated without an actual war, it started in 1938. For us English people it started on 3 September 1939. Indeed I was once mistaken enough to write a book called *The Origins of the Second World War* which worked up to 3 September 1939, which was the day Great Britain declared war on Germany. In my last paragraph I realised I had been writing on the wrong subject and finished up by saying: 'What I have described is

German troops crossing into Czechoslovakia near Heidmühle, 1938

the origins of a minor conflict in Europe, the effects of which have been lost without trace and were only a preliminary to the real world conflict which came later.'

At any rate I thought I would try to present it in different terms, accepting that there were a series of wars which seemed of course very serious and great to those who were involved in them. The actual Polish war for instance lasted a fortnight so far as the serious fighting was concerned but it was a great war while it was on and in its effects for the Poles.

The war between France and Germany, in which British troops were involved to a lesser extent in May to June 1940 lasted for something like at most six weeks—from any dynamic point of view a fortnight. The Germans in conquering Europe between 1939 and 1940 suffered fewer casualities than they had suffered, say, during the battle of the Somme in 1916.

These were all preliminaries and no more than this. From June 1940 until June 1941 there was virtually peace in Europe and for that matter generally in the world. There were minor aggressions, there were minor conflicts and there was a running undercurrent of conflict. When I say that there was no great war I mean predominently that there was no land war, apart from a very short-lived engagement in Greece. British troops were not in conflict with the Germans at all in Europe during that period and only to a very slight extent even in North Africa.

The only striking episode in this period of British history was a war between England and Italy in North Africa, which although a very dramatic and sensational affair had little relevance to the world struggle. Unlike the first world war where we still have doubts what the issues were, whether it really was a conscious struggle for the mastery of Europe or of the world, the second world war had a more defined character. Some of the great powers possessing empires or protected zones of their own could derive adequate resources from what they possessed. That was true of the United States; the whole, really, of the American continent was America's and nobody else's. This was also true of the British Empire and of the French Empire.

Two of the great industrial countries of the world did not possess such zones, they were short of resources and back-

Motorised Nazi troops entering Prague

ground. Quite apart from other things—their nationalist feeling, and their political aims such as German Nazism—they were discontented with their lot and were seeking to break into the monopoly of the other great powers. This is a pattern which occurred all through the 1930s. On the one hand the contented empires; on the other the discontented aggrieved powers Germany and Japan.

Japan throughout the 1930s was aspiring to make first China and then the whole of the Far East, as they called it, The Greater Asia Co-Prosperity Sphere. When people use the term 'co-prosperity' of course it does not mean it is going to benefit those they conquer; it means it is going to benefit the con-

The Premier's triumphal return from Munich. Chamberlain
speaking into the microphone as he addresses the
crowd at Heston Airport, 30 September 1938

querors. Co-prosperity is just a name for grabbing other people's resources, though it sounds very impressive.

In the same way, German leaders and particularly Hitler looked forward to a greater Germany with greater resources and more land. Essentially they aimed to break the structure of monopoly which penned them in. This is quite different from saying that they necessarily aspired to world war, still less to world conquest. Germany and Japan sought a secure recognised place at the table of the great. They wanted to sit down with the great empires as equals. Of course when people say that, they always want to be superiors too.

One of the things which historians have seen more clearly with the passing of the years is how closely the European

German troops entering Danzig, September 1939

Hitler walking beside the Vistula in Poland, 12 September 1939

question and the Far Eastern question were linked. For instance the policy of appeasement which Chamberlain followed from 1937 to 1939 was largely designed to get Europe settled so that the British forces could move to the Far East and resist Japan. On the other side, the reluctance of the United States to get involved in the European theatre sprang to a great extent from the consciousness in Washington that the Far East was their most pressing concern and one where, with the

European countries too busy in Europe, they had no associates.

Therefore, it seems to me the story of the second world war begins as a practical proposition in June 1940. In June 1940 the readjustment of Europe was complete. It had been achieved at fantastically low cost in men and in equipment. There had never been an imperial conquest which had been achieved so easily as the way in which Hitler established German domination over Europe. In June 1940 Germany dominated the entire continent of Europe, either directly through her power or indirectly, as with the few remaining neutrals, by her influence and requirements. Indeed you can go further and say Europe was united for the only time in its history and there seemed

In the historic railway carriage at Compiègne the Germans (Keitel *left*) lay down terms for the armistice of 22 June 1940

Chinese marching along the Great Wall

little likelihood that this situation could be reversed from within Europe. We know that in fact any resistance in Europe, although sometimes very honourable, was ineffective in pushing the Germans back.

The only remnant of this earlier war, the war which had started in 1939 and terminated in the railway carriage at Compiègne when the French signed the armistice, was that Great Britain remained in the war. Indeed this was the basic contribution which Great Britain made to the world war that came later. As Stalin put it, at a much later time, the Russians gave blood, the Americans provided money, the British provided time. They ensured that something like a war-like situation would remain.

After the attempt by Hitler to invade Great Britain in August–September 1940, neither side could strike decisively against the other. There were ineffective bombing raids. That again sounds ironical to anyone who lived through the blitz but compared to any real heavy air bombardment, the blitz carried no weight and achieved no result.

The one factor which might have changed the war and which threatened Great Britain and brought her to the brink of defeat was the struggle in the Atlantic between the German

War in North Africa: Italian prisoners leaving Bardia for the base camp January 1941

133

German troops' victory parade in Berlin after the fall of France, July 1940

U-boats against the British convoys and this provided a link with the war that was to come after. Otherwise British and German armies were not fighting.

In 1941 when we in this country were already facing fairly limited rations, much of the German army was demobilised and German munitions production was cut down. There was a feeling that the war was over, yet it was not over because of the

'Eagle Day': Göring directs the air offensive against England, summer 1940

'Sea Lion': Hitler's invasion barges waiting in Boulogne
harbour, 1940

138

The Battle of the Atlantic, 1941

theoretical fact that Great Britain maintained the war and this was one of the things which imposed a strain upon Hitler. He could not say 'The war is finished.' He often talked about how he would like to make peace with Great Britain but he never attempted it seriously and probably any attempts he made would have been rebuffed.

One of the fascinating topics still well worth studying is why did the British keep going so well? I do not mean to say effectively. They were not having any effect against Hitler at this time until they could bring a greater war to bear. Why did they hold out when their cause seemed impossible, when everybody said 'Well, Hitler can't invade Great Britain but then Great Britain will never be able to defeat Hitler'? What kept them going? Some hope for the future? I often think an echo of the past, a memory of earlier times when they stood alone against Napoleon, dragging on for ten years. In the end something would come right.

What should Hitler do faced with this position that Europe was his? Should he just rest on his laurels? It is fairly clear that he anticipated further struggle. It maybe also that having once mobilised his army he felt he must use it, and we know that after twelve months of deliberation and preparation, Hitler's decision was to invade Russia.

Here is one of the very rare cases in how a war begins. There are wars which have been planned in the sense that countries have built up their armies and envisaged that there would be a conflict. For instance when the Germans built a navy against Great Britain before 1914, they assumed that one of these days there would be a naval war. But here Hitler and his staff sat down months beforehand and said first of all 15 May and then, with weather and other things interfering, 22 June 1941, as the day they would start their next war. It is very rare that there should be such an absolute precise timetable. Why 22 June? Not because there was anything dramatic happening then but because it would fit in with their timetable. Unlike most wars, unlike I am prepared to say Hitler's earlier wars, this was a war of absolutely clear cut determination with no argument, with no hesitations.

Why did Hitler do it? People have talked about this a lot, I think too much. Some people say he wanted to destroy com-

140

Parade in Red Square, 1940

munism. Some that he wanted to acquire great stretches of Russia, what he called 'Lebensraum', living space. Others say in more practical terms that he feared the ultimate strength of Russia. He argued 'We are the stronger now but as soon as Russia gets the stronger, the Russians will attack us.'

We have no idea what Russia's intentions were, except of course a clear cut intention to survive. There is no indication at all of preparations to attack Germany or even to take precautions. Stalin we know was absolutely fixed on the doctrine that until Great Britain had been defeated, Germany would not attack him.

When we look at the records it is clear why the decision was taken. The German generals and Hitler were absolutely confident they would win, so why not go ahead? How simple it would be. In an earlier stage there had been arguments about whether they should attack France. Many of the generals doubted whether France could be defeated. Hitler insisted it was possible and it was. The French army was supposed to be

Hitler and Molotov negotiating. November 1940

Planning the invasion of Russia: Hitler with Keitel and von Brauchitsch
(early 1941)

the greatest in Europe. If France could be defeated within a
month, Russia could be defeated within a few weeks. The very
practical, simple, straightforward answer to the question 'Why
did Hitler invade Russia?' is because he was confident he
would win and with this all serious threat to the German
domination of Europe would disappear for ever. Indeed he said
as much very often: 'Once the British have lost all hope in
Russia they will make peace and the German empire will be
secure.'

At the same time Hitler was becoming, as victors always do,
as Napoleon did for that matter but even more so, more confident and greedier with each success, and even before he
attacked Russia he was making the next jump. Earlier he had
said: 'The final battle for the world will be between Europe, led

143

German pioneer troops crossing frontier bridge into Russia, 22 June 1941

of course by Germany, and the United States, but it will not happen in my time. It will happen in a hundred years time.'

After he had conquered France he still said 'The battle between Europe and America will happen in my time, it will happen in twenty years', but the moment he had decided that Russia could be eliminated in the early days of 1941, he said 'The battle for the world will start in 1942 or thereabouts. We want to get Russia out of the way and acquire Russia's resources, and then for the great war against America.'

There is no doubt why the Germans went to war with Russia; they went to war with the absolute blind confidence that they would win. It would be such an easy war that it was inconceivable to turn it down.

This was a decisive step towards world war. It was a more decisive step than the Germans expected of course because Russia survived instead of being defeated within a month as everyone had expected, as the German generals had expected, as the British general staff had expected, as the American army had expected. Germany was faced with, if not world war, at any rate a conflict of the greatest size and with it the implication that German power would not necessarily be sustained on this level.

We must also bring in the other side. It is not possible to understand the origins of how the second world war actually came into being without considering the similar story of Japan in the Far East. Here too the Japanese had great successes, they had successes before the war in which they established their control over most of the coast of China and most of the Chinese ports. Here again there was a parallel with Great Britain; just as Great Britain kept a war going by merely existing so Nationalist China kept a war going by merely existing. The Chinese did virtually no fighting against Japan between 1938 or early 1939 and the end of the world war but they were still theoretically in existence. Incidentally China did not declare war on Japan until after Pearl Harbor but there they were and this tempted Japan to go further along the coast. Moreover with the collapse of the European powers and their empires, the Dutch empire and the French empire, these were wide open. The Japanese saw the opportunity to break the ring and acquire raw materials for themselves.

In the background the factor which more than anything else shaped and conditioned the second world war was the United States, indisputably at that time the greatest industrial power in the world, a power with a stake in European affairs and also in Far Eastern affairs, a power torn between the overwhelming desire of a great many of its people to keep out of war and on the other hand a similar desire to assert American principles of democracy and of what one could call free trade or more truly free investment for American money. That was the basis of America's liberal economy.

It was very much in America's interest to keep Great Britain going, not only interest in the economic sense but interest in the strategic sense. Ever since the Declaration of Independence in

145

Pearl Harbor, December 7th, 1941

1776, Great Britain had willingly or not supplied a strategical buffer between the United States and Europe. It was for this reason to a great extent that the United States had entered the first world war in 1917.

More than this, Great Britain now represented the only way in which American power if it were going to be reasserted, could get back into Europe. From very early on in the war, American strategists, envisaging that there would be a war between Germany and the United States, pointed to Great Britain as their impregnable aircraft carrier, from which American troops could get into Europe. The struggle in the Atlantic therefore directly involved the United States.

For American battleships and destroyers the second world war began a long time before Pearl Harbor. It began in the summer of 1941 when Germany and the United States were unofficially at war in the Atlantic. On the other side America was following a similar policy of holding back Japan. Here again we can point to a precise moment when the second world war in the Far East became inevitable, when it was decided on. This was not a Japanese decision; it was an American decision.

In August 1941 the United States government imposed a total embargo on supplies to Japan, particularly supplies of oil and of credits. From that moment Japan was doomed either to surrender at discretion or to go to war. The Japanese had six months' supply of oil. Actually as usual they overstated their distress. They could have lasted out for a year or two but the doctrine was 'We have only got six months—before that we must break through the ring.' In anything but a technical sense the United States had declared war on Japan by thus attempting to close the ring.

By the autumn of 1941 therefore the situation was changing in some ways for the better, in some ways for the worse. On the one hand the German predominance in Europe which had seemed so complete and so unshakeable in the summer of 1941 was now gravely threatened.

In June 1941 everybody virtually, there were a few exceptions of whom I was one, said 'Russia will be defeated'. By the autumn most strategical experts were still shaking their heads and saying 'Well it has been tougher for the Germans than we expected but Russia is bound to collapse.' By November it

150 American mothers demonstrate in Washington against passage of the
Lend Lease Bill, 13 February 1941

149

looked as if Russia was going to survive and there was a short period when the Russians themselves thought they had already won and Stalin was talking about complete victory in 1942. This was a fantastic turn of events.

The other aspect of this was the tense situation in the Far East. Did the Americans, did Roosevelt, deliberately turn the screw on Japan in the confidence that Japan would go to war?

We shall never be able to answer this absolutely clearly. I am inclined to think 'No'. I am inclined to think that until October 1941 or perhaps early November, the Americans still thought that the Japanese, faced with this rigid blockade, cut off from their oil, would compromise, would draw back from some of their conquests and would seek a settlement, not quite a surrender but at any rate a withdrawal, with the Americans.

The Japanese on their side had no hesitation. They had decided they were going to break the ring. Where they hesitated was exactly how to do it, but we know that quite a long

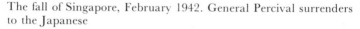

The fall of Singapore, February 1942. General Percival surrenders to the Japanese

Japanese troops storm Kuala Lumpur

time before Pearl Harbor they had decided that the American fleet must be eliminated.

Hitler may have talked about dominating the world. The Japanese had no such fantasies; they wanted to establish The Far Eastern Co-Prosperity Sphere and with that they would be content.

They undertook the attack on Pearl Harbor on 7 December 1941. This was not linked up with the European war. In fact the Japanese got their timing absolutely wrong because on 7 December the Soviet armies began a counter-offensive.

Maybe if the Japanese had hesitated one more day they would have pulled back and realised they had missed the bus. As it was they started the world war—not quite. Hitler finally launched the second world war by his declaration of war on America. Why did he do this? Why did he give this most

151

Landing on Christmas Island in the Pacific, cheering Japanese forces in an occupied battery, February 1942

extraordinary assistance to the allies? We shall never know.

Perhaps that marks the moment when the second world war began but perhaps not. Churchill certainly thought it was later, because he said after the battle of El Alamein in October 1942 'This may not be the beginning of the end but it is the end of the beginning.'

6
THE COLD WAR

The Cold War

I suppose 'How the Cold War Began' is rather a contradictory title because the essence of the Cold War is that it was a war which was expected to begin but never actually began. However I suppose we know roughly what we have in mind by the term 'Cold War'. It applies to some parts of the international relations between Soviet Russia and the United States in the thirty years or so since the war—periods of tension.

Now international tension is nothing like so unusual as people imagine. Indeed the normal relation of sovereign powers is to distrust each other and to pursue rival ambitions. All through the nineteenth century for instance, Great Britain was running in rivalry to either Russia or France or in the early twentieth century to Germany. Nor is it unusual for former allies to quarrel. In fact the normal thing at the end of any great war is that the alliances break up and they fall out.

In 1815 England and Austria, the victors, made an alliance with France, their former enemy, against Russia their former ally who had indeed delivered Europe from the conqueror, and if something the same happened in 1945 this was only to be expected.

There were however and still are deeper elements than the normal rivalry and distrust which great powers show for one another. For one thing Russia, even when a great power, has never been fully accepted as part of Europe. There has always been an assumption that Russia was just on the fringe of

154

Europe. She was indeed quite often in the nineteenth century referred to as an Asiatic and almost an inferior power.

In 1856 after the Crimean war when somebody objected that the terms imposed on Russia were very harsh, much harsher incidentally than those imposed by Bismarck on France in 1871, Palmerston replied 'Well what can an Asiatic power expect?'

When Russia has claimed that she should be treated on the same level, has the same rights to make claims as other great powers, this produces not only indignation but surprise.

In 1945 for instance at the end of the second world war, when the victors were first speculating as to how things should be shared out, the British who were hoping still to maintain the whole of their empire and their domination of the Mediterranean, were astonished to learn that Russian statesmen hoped to acquire Libya. If the Americans had come along and said 'We should like a colony in the Mediterranean and have decided that Libya should be the one', nobody would have minded. It would have been regarded as the normal thing for a great power to do. For Russia to do it was an outrage, an uncivilised, an Asiatic thing.

Similary in 1945 the British still controlled both ends of the Mediterranean, the Straits of Gibraltar and the Suez Canal and this was said to be essential to their national security, although the Mediterranean, heaven knows, is quite a long way from this country. The Russians said that they would like to control the Straits of Bosphorus and the Dardenelles. This would give them an outlet—it was a good deal more important to them than Gibraltar and Suez were to the British. Immediately the talk began of Russian aggression but of course this was strengthened by many other things.

There is a greater division of ideology between Russia and the western powers than between any of the western powers themselves. This did not begin with Communism; it began with the religious cleavage. The Russians have the Orthodox church and are very arrogant about it. Their church is officially called 'the Orthodox Church', so what does that leave the rest of us with? I suppose we are all some kind of heretics, second rate Christians, compared to the truly Orthodox. Add to this, Marxism which again claims to know all the secrets of the

155

Crowded vespers at Trapezny cathedral

economic system. Russian statesmen, writers, have a determination to be right, a self-confidence which is asserted the more because others by no means always recognise it.

There are considerations of a more practical nature. Russia in the nineteenth century had great conflicts with Great Britain particularly in the Middle East. With the Russian revolution there followed a very great increase in the cleavage when, a thing often forgotten in the west, Great Britain and France, with some cooperation from America, conducted wars of intervention on a very considerable scale against the Bolshevik government.

What the British and French did in 1919 was very much what the old reactionary powers had done against France in 1793. In this case the wars of intervention were a failure and though they did not provoke an actual counter-war on the part of Russia, they certainly created hostility on both sides. Throughout the inter-war period there has been this antagonism and a deep-based suspicion. Here again suspicion is the normal relationship between great powers. That is particularly true of course of the military advisers. After all it is the job of generals and admirals and air marshals to prepare for wars. They can only prepare for war at all sensibly if they envisage an antagonist and when they cannot see an obvious antagonist then they find unlikely antagonists.

In the 1920s for instance when Germany had almost ceased to exist as a military power, and Russia had been forgotten, the British air staff in order to justify a large air force invented the French peril. They argued that because France had a large air force, this was inevitably bound to be used against Great Britain and therefore we must build a large air force in return. The large air force was not built but the alarm was sounded.

I was reading just the other day a fascinating account of American military and strategic plans between the wars, at a time when neither Germany nor Russia was a danger. The American strategists had to justify themselves so they sounded the alarm that America as always was in danger. After all if your country is not in danger you would not have an army or an air force or a navy and that would never do for the people who are running the army, the air force and the navy. So what did the army strategists in America discover in the middle of the

158

Foreign intervention in Russia: British troops parade in Vladivostock, 1918

1920s? They discovered that a country called Red, which was in fact the United Kingdom, was preparing to invade White, which was the United States, with an army of 8 million men in order to destroy the whole of American industry. This was not some fantasy of a novelist. It was the work of a serious strategical planner, trained in the staff colleges and sitting down in genuine alarm that any day a new Armada might be sighted crossing the Atlantic, landing in Canada, and then 8 million British troops marching I suppose on Chicago. 'Ah,' you may say, 'a fantasy; they didn't take many steps about it'. In fact

159

Stalin, Truman and Churchill, Potsdam, 17 July 1945

Churchill at the ruined Chancellery, Berlin, 16 July 1945

they did. The Americans recast their strategical thinking entirely in face of the supposed danger from the British on the one side and Japan on the other, and the reason why in 1941 the Americans put Germany first was simply that they had put the other European danger—England—first fifteen or twenty years before.

The suspicion and rivalry between Soviet Russia and the great powers turned then on the historical record, on Russia's

161

Atlee, Truman and
Stalin at Potsdam,
July 1945

162

geographical position and most of all on the transformation of Russian society which we call the Bolshevik Revolution.

No such cleavage had existed in western civilisation since the time of the French Revolution and even at the time of the French Revolution the cleavage was, though fierce, relatively short. The cleavage which started in 1917 between the state which claimed to be Communist and the countries which called themselves 'Democratic' or 'Capitalistic' or 'Liberal' has endured to the present day. It may be argued that the cleavage is now less, that all western countries are becoming more communised, at any rate run by great corporations and

Soviet soldiers going home from Germany, 1945

164

The Berlin Wall

not by individual enterprise, perhaps becoming less democratic too. It could hardly I think be argued that Soviet Russia is becoming more democratic. It is possible however that she is becoming less rigidly communistic. Nevertheless the cleavage is still there and I sometimes think that what people in the west dislike about the Soviet Russia or what many people dislike about Soviet Russia is not the bad things in Soviet Russia but the good ones. It is not so much that people dislike the labour camps, the suppression of freedom of thought, the constant thought control, the secret police. What many people really dislike is that Russia has no capitalists and no private landlords. Marxism—which is after all a perfectly legitimate and coherent system of economic thought—is now used as a term of abuse and it is supposed that anyone who is a Marxist can hardly be British at all, even though Marxism was after all invented in the British Museum. No system of thought is more fully integrally British than Marxism but this is not how people think of it nowadays.

How far this crusade of ideas still persists it is difficult to say.

In 1918, though the western powers wanted to grab Russian territory as well, there is no doubt that they regarded Bolshevism as a really barbaric idea. Now I think this is confined to theoreticians—most practical people take it as an oddity and not very much more—but insofar as Russia is a socialist state, this still provides a cleavage and a cause of tension which can flare up in the most unlikely places.

These however are not the practical considerations. At the end of the second world war there was a suspicion on both sides simply beginning with the very extent of the victory. Ever since 1941 the victors, the three great powers, had been held together by the need to defeat Germany and this need imposed tremendous demands on them. Despite whatever people have said, in my opinion none of the three great powers had any reserves about waging the war against Germany. They put the defeat of Hitler and Nazi Germany above everything else. Then suddenly, you see, Nazi Germany was defeated, suddenly Hitler was not there. The danger which had forced them together had disappeared and although they talked at their Potsdam meeting, and later of the possibility of a revived German danger, the fact is that the German danger has, I

Lifting the Berlin Blockade, the first road convoy arrives, 14 May 1949

think, disappeared. I did not think that for a long time. I went on for a long time after the war being apprehensive of a revived Germany but I now admit that Germany has become a pacific country, thoroughly integrated into western democratic ways. Equally true of course in the Far East, Japan has ceased to be a political and military danger although in a sense she is still an economic rival, as Germany is for that matter.

A wide range of misunderstandings began in 1945, some of which have continued to the present day. For instance the Russians had had the most terrible experiences, twenty million dead, nor was this the first time that such a thing had happened

The Soviet ship *Anosov* returning to Russia from Cuba with missiles and
missile-transporters visible on deck

169

to them. In fact Russia has been invaded by one European country or another five times since the beginning of the nineteenth century. By Napoleon in 1812, by the British and French in 1856, by the Germans in 1914 to 1917, by the British and French again in 1919 and by the Germans in 1941. Russia has never invaded Europe except in answer to the conqueror and one can say as a liberator. Russian troops came to Berlin in 1945, just as they had come to Paris in 1814, not as conquerors but simply to drive the conquerors back or so it appears in retrospect. At the time men feared that they had come as conquerors.

We shall never know in our lifetime and perhaps we shall never know what were the secret counsels of the Soviet leaders in 1945 or indeed now. All those who claim to know about Soviet policy, Kremlinologists they are called, guess; that is all you can do about Russia. I differ from them but only because I guess slightly differently. No one has any solid information about Soviet policy from inside.

There are many who think that in 1945, Stalin and his hordes wanted to sweep right across Europe. In my opinion and I am as entitled to my opinion as others are, this was not the case. Soviet policy wanted security: the defeat of Germany, and then the building up of a ring of satellite states which would ensure Soviet Russia's security.

Far from wanting the spread of Communism, and this is something we know from the evidence before us, Stalin deliberately prevented the possible victory of Communism in both Italy and France and it is now, I may say, much against the will of the Soviet leaders that Communism is growing in strength in Italy and to a lesser extent in France. My guess is that the last thing the Soviet leaders want is to see the success of European Communist parties, because if any great European country went Communist it would eclipse Soviet Russia.

This, however, is not how it seemed to others at the time. The extensions of Russian power into Czechoslovakia and Poland were deplored by Great Britain and still more by the United States, even though the United States's policy and influence were being extended by different means into western Europe. How did western Europe recover and be saved from Communism? By American economic aid because America

170

Czechoslovakia, February 1948. Klement Gottwald the
Premier addresses Communist mass rally in the Old
City Square, Prague

attached importance to preserving western Europe as what it still is—an American outpost. Europe was divided into on the one hand American outposts and on the other hand Soviet outposts—neither possibly with any aggressive intention.

There was I think one period of genuine Cold War. I mean with one of the powers planning to take aggressive moves to drive the other back, not necessarily by war but by overwhelming pressure, and that was in the years when the United States alone possessed nuclear weapons. We know quite well that from the moment the atomic bombs were dropped on Hiroshima and Nagasaki, American policy became tougher. There was a time when President Truman and others were envisaging that Russia would be pushed back to her 1939 frontiers. After all President Truman who succeeded Roosevelt only by the accident of Roosevelt's death, said on the outbreak of war between Russia and Germany in 1941, 'We should stand aside and let each of the two scoundrels cut each others' throats, supporting whichever happens to be the weaker at the moment.' So he showed little appreciation for Soviet Russia as an ally and I would speculate also that the Berlin airlift, that is to say the Russian blockade of Berlin, was in part an answer to this atomic alarm.

It is worth bearing in mind that the Berlin airlift could not have been continued for 24 hours unless the control towers, all manned by Soviet observers and operators, had been kept going, so that it was the Russians who really conducted the Berlin airlift as it were or patronised it.

The world situation undoubtedly changed when the Russians acquired nuclear secrets of their own, secrets I think which owed a great deal more to the work of Soviet scientists than to British or American defectors. From this moment there began a balance, sometimes called the balance of terror.

As with other weapons it is not necessary to be as strong if you are on the defensive as on the offensive. In the second world war it was said that the offensive had to be five times as strong as the defensive if it were to succeed and something the same can be said about nuclear weapons. Russia until recently has not been as strong in nuclear weapons as the United States but has been strong enough to pose some threat and in all these years although there have been apprehensions, there has been

Armed police marching past the new Czechoslovak government, Prague, 1 March 1948

only one alarm, in my opinion a mistaken one. This was called the Cuban missile crisis of 1962, often represented as an American victory. What it secured certainly was the withdrawal of Soviet rocket bases from Cuba but the Americans paid a price. They acknowledged Cuba's independence, and never repeated the attempt to destroy it as they had done in the Bay of Pigs affair. Cuba is really under a Soviet guarantee to the present day. Altogether an interesting experience of how near one could go to war.

Other Russian activities come, in my opinion, under the

heading of defensive answers, answers which were very tiresome to those upon whom they were inflicted. There was a tendency for each side to nibble, hoping that there would be cracks in the lines of division. This was true in regard to Czechoslovakia in 1948, it was true in a different way in regard to Hungary in 1956.

The last time I saw President Beneš of Czechoslovakia which was in 1947, he said to me 'I have always hoped that Czechoslovakia would be a link, a hyphen between the western powers and the eastern powers. If now east and west quarrel, Czechoslovakia must go with Russia.' When I asked him why, he said 'Because it is our only secure defence against the Germans.' This is a theme which is sometimes forgotten in the west. Maybe the alarm is now artificial but it certainly existed at that time.

The Hungarian case is more contentious. The Hungarian revolution or rising could be depicted as a movement of good democrats. It could also be depicted as having been captured by those who looked back to the fascist, aristocratic, clerical-run Hungary of the inter-war years. Though the Soviet intervention was a move in the Cold War, it was specifically designed to ensure that this did not turn into hot war.

What is happening in other parts of the world is a different matter. Though we can look forward—for some years—to a reasonable balance between Russia and the United States, I think the most likely warlike events will sound like echoes from the ninteenth century. Wars of liberation have been fought in the last 30 years: the liberation of Vietnam, the liberation of Algeria and it may well be, though much regretted, wars of liberation in Africa, but these will not deeply affect the world balance. The Americans talked a lot of nonsense about the domino theory and asserted that if Vietnam went, the whole of South East Asia would be lost. So far the only consequence of the defeat of America in Vietnam is that the reunited Vietnam is stronger and more independent than it was before.

On the whole we have done pretty well since the war in not producing any great men. Great men are splendid in war time, maybe essential, but they can be dangerous in peace time. Great men have produced wars as Napoleon did. All the world statesmen now are rather humdrum secondary people who are

174

unlikely to aspire to be world conquerors. The one force which still aspires to conquer the world is the planning staffs. They will produce the alarms and frights.

People often ask historians to tell them about the future. Heaven knows it is difficult enough to know about the past. The historian is no more competent than anyone else to foretell the future. In fact in many ways he is less competent because he understands the infinite variety of what might happen. When people ask me 'Will there be another world war?' I am inclined to answer 'If men behave in the future as they have done in the past there will be another war.' But of course it is always possible that men will behave differently.

As a personal hunch I think it is unlikely and that there will be a third world war. One day the deterrent will fail to deter.

OVERLEAF
Anti-Communist demonstrations, Budapest. (1956)

Index